SO YOU THINK YOU'RE A
DIE-HARD

FAN

SO YOU THINK YOU'RE A DIE-HARD

DIE-HARD

Tiger FAN

BY JOE FALLS

CONTEMPORARY
BOOKS, INC.

CHICAGO ▪ NEW YORK

Library of Congress Cataloging-in-Publication Data

Falls, Joe.
  So you think you're a die-hard Tiger fan.

  1. Detroit Tigers (Baseball team)—History.
2. Detroit Tigers (Baseball team)—Miscellanea.
I. Title.
GV875.D6F343   1986   796.357′64′0977434   86-2330
ISBN 0-8092-5074-8

All photos courtesy of the *Detroit News* except the following: those on
pages xv, xvi, 8, 9, 11, 14, 16, 17 (bottom), 18, 21, 22, 23, 24, 25 (top), 30,
32, 41, 44, 51, 55, 62, 63 (top), 75, 76, 84, 86, 91, 101, 112, 121, 122, 133, and
142 courtesy of the Detroit Tigers; those on pages 43, 49, 66, 67, and 72
courtesy of Irwin Cohen.

Copyright © 1986 by Joe Falls
All rights reserved
Published by Contemporary Books, Inc.
180 North Michigan Avenue, Chicago, Illinois 60601
Manufactured in the United States of America
Library of Congress Catalog Card Number: 86-2330
International Standard Book Number: 0-8092-5074-8

Published simultaneously in Canada by Beaverbooks, Ltd.
195 Allstate Parkway, Valleywood Business Park
Markham, Ontario L3R 4T8 Canada

This book is dedicated to John E. Fetzer.

CONTENTS

Ernie Harwell, voice of the Tigers.

FOREWORD

Remember when the game-winning double into the right-field corner with two out in the bottom of the ninth inning was the thing we all went home talking about? We are into so many other things in sports—money, drugs, and drinking—that we sometimes forget the joy of our games.

Here is a book that talks about the joy of our games.

It is a celebration of baseball—a celebration of the Detroit Tigers.

Joe Falls has covered the Tigers for 32 years. He has seen them in their good times and their bad times. He has written about the good and the bad. Sometimes people agree with him, sometimes they don't. But Joe has never lost his enthusiasm for baseball.

He loves the game and it shows in his writing.

He loves the grass, the scoreboard in center field, the light towers—and he goes home talking about the double into the right-field corner that sent home the winning runs with two out in the bottom of the ninth inning.

He knows the second baseman of the Tigers from 1924—Charlie Gehringer—just as he knows the second baseman in 1986—Lou Whitaker. He writes about them all in a light and airy way that makes the game a joy for all of us.

If you read on, you might find out what Sparky Anderson likes for breakfast and what his five favorite swimming pools are in the major leagues. You might even find out about barber shops, elevators, and the longest home run in Detroit history.

So you think you're a die-hard Tiger fan? Here's where you can find out.

Ernie Harwell
January 1, 1986

Will everyone please rise as Bob Taylor sings the National Anthem?

INTRODUCTION

Nowhere do they burn police cars, close down the bleachers, and drop cherry bombs in the face of the rightfielder.

They do it in my town.

Detroit.

My town is a tough town but a good town. They care around here. They care about their ball club. They've been caring for more than 100 years.

Our fans can get out of control and it gets scary. There is no room for rowdyism in the ballpark. But they want to be part of the action. It is not enough for them to sit and watch the players perform. The feelings go very deep in Detroit. Baseball is an important part of their lives. It seems as if the Tigers have been in their lives as long as they can remember. They know more about Ernie Harwell than Mayor Young. They grew up playing the game in their backyards and on the streets and at the corner lots. They can tell you that Dick Bartell never should have held that ball in the 1940 World Series against the Reds. They can tell you that Kirk Gibson drives his truck to the ballpark. They can tell you that Mickey Lolich used to ride in on his motorcycle.

That's the way it is in my town—baseball is very important to the people.

Nobody is storming the Bastille. It's much more important. The fans are celebrating the 1968 pennant.

When the Tigers are winning, it's like a citywide picnic in Detroit. There is no better place to be than in the ballpark on a summer's night or on a warm weekend afternoon. That's Tom Brookens, slightly bowlegged, patting his glove at third base and getting ready for the next pitch. You can see that Jack Morris is very serious. His face is hard, without expression, as he looks to Lance Parrish for the sign. Sparky Anderson is spitting out sunflower seeds in the dugout.

It is a marvelous feeling when the Tigers are winning. When they start losing, look out. A frustration sets in and sets in quickly. The fans can become unruly. They once threw the back of a chair at Roger Maris of the Yankees. It was into the face of Ken Harrelson that they dropped their cherry bomb from the upper deck in right field. They hit umpire Bill Summers with a whiskey bottle on Opening Day and knocked him to the ground. When George Hendrick, the Oakland centerfielder, made the final catch to end the playoffs against the Tigers in 1972, he had to step around a wine bottle to pull down Tony Taylor's drive in deep center. The bottle, of course, was empty.

A pitcher from the Oakland A's—Paul Lindblad—used to come into our ballpark with a minesweeper and spend his afternoons seeing what he could find in the outfield grass. He came up with an assortment of nuts and bolts and ball bearings and two spent bullets.

All of these things are true and they are hurtful if you care about this town or this team. These are the things that many people choose to remember about Detroit. They remember the negative things. You think they know this city gives more money, per capita, to charity than any city in the United States? But they'll tell you about that burning police car after the final game of the 1984 World Series.

Pennants, anyone?

"I've got to get back to the zoo."

All of this is distressing because Detroit is a great baseball town.

They don't give you fireworks or dancing chickens or even sauerkraut for your hot dogs in Detroit.

They give you baseball.

They wear the same uniforms they wore when Hank Greenberg was blasting them into section 14. They play on grass, and, if you're lucky, the post in front of you won't block out too much of the second baseman. When you walk into Tiger Stadium, you are nowhere else in the world but in a ballpark.

You can smell the hot dogs on the grill and you can feel the damp chill of the old concrete walls as you walk through the clammy corridors beneath the stands. The stands loom large with the light towers reaching into the skies. The dugouts are half-buried in the ground, the way dugouts should be. You can never take your eyes off the players when they emerge from the third-base dugout in their creamy-white uniforms and trot out to take their places in the field. We never get tired of this sight. It is a new experience for us each time.

Whenever this city has fallen on hard times, the people of Detroit have turned to the ball club to help them through.

Come on out, Sparky. Things will get better in 1986.

When the Great Depression hit in the 1930s and the auto industry was struggling for survival, the people turned out to see Mickey Cochrane and his men win two straight pennants and beat the Chicago Cubs in the 1935 World Series. Men were selling apples on street corners. Others gathered at the gates of their auto plants, trying to keep warm over fires built in oil cans, wondering when they might go to work again.

When the Tigers started winning, the people began flocking to the corner of Michigan and Trumbull. They came on streetcars and they came on foot. They had something to do with their afternoons. They could forget their troubles for the moment. They had a reason to feel good about something—a reason to feel proud. At least Detroit was the best in something, even if it was only baseball.

The same thing happened in 1968. The city had been ravaged by the riot in '67 and Detroit was an armed camp in the spring of '68. Everyone feared what would happen when the streets started heating up again in the summer.

Suddenly, here was Willie Horton putting one into the upper left-field deck and Denny McLain—darling Denny—pouring his high, hard

"Why, what makes you think we're Tiger fans?"

one past Boog Powell of the Orioles. People put away their weapons and began gathering around their radios and TV sets. You could walk through whole alleys—from street to street—and listen to Ernie Harwell's voice through the open windows and never miss a pitch of the game. Once more there was a reason to feel good—to feel proud. It is foolhardy to say the Tigers saved the city in the summer of 1968, but who has a better explanation for what happened?

This is a city that embraced a young man named Mark Fidrych and turned his appearances in the ballpark into religious experiences.

This is the city that booed Sparky Anderson, then stood up and applauded him, and didn't know there was a difference.

This is a city that shouted so many obscenities that the boss of the Tigers had to take away their privilege of sitting in the cheaper seats.

This is my city.

Detroit.

I wouldn't trade it for two New Yorks and a Chicago to be named at a later date.

Not a bad hat trick, young lady.

"Yeah, buddy, dey plump when ya cook 'em."

PART I
THE OLD BALLPARK

THE AGE OF INNOCENCE

They once asked outfielder Davy Jones of the Tigers the secret of his success. He said: "I don't have a secret. I just have a Limburger sandwich and two bottles of beer before I go to bed every night."

These were the early 1900s. An innocent time in Detroit.

Henry Ford worked out of a little shack in Dearborn and not many people were taking his new invention very seriously. The baseball team played at the intersection of Michigan and Trumbull avenues and the field was known as Bennett Park. Home plate was set down out in the present right-field area. The field was located on the site of the old Haymarket, which had originally been paved with cobblestones. Only a few inches of loam were spread over the cobblestones, so the balls took some weird bounces. Whenever the fielders muffed a ball, they would say: "It hit another cobble."

Everything was pretty plain by today's standards. The clubhouses were little more than run-down shanties. The players knew nothing of whirlpool baths, electrotherapy, skilled trainers—or even hot water. They waited in line for the single cold shower to be vacated. They used yesterday's towel to dry today's body.

The uniforms were often damp and smelly. Ty Cobb recalled: "Sometimes they'd be out-and-out wet when we put them on. They were jammed into containers after a

1

Recreation Park (Brush & Brady) on July 4, 1887.

game in their natural sweat-soaked state and they seldom saw a laundry. We'd wear them until they were a grimy disgrace."

Nobody complained. Nobody knew better.

The pitchers were allowed to doctor up the ball any way they wanted, applying coatings of talcum, slippery elm, licorice, or just plain spit. Nobody wore sunglasses or had webbing in his gloves. The bats looked as if they were purchased at drugstore sales. They had no padding on the walls or cinder tracks warning the players they were headed for the walls.

Benefits? Once in a while the manager might buy his players a beer.

Agents? The players were lucky if they got the same salary from year to year even if they batted over .300. They got less than a dollar a day in meal money.

Nobody had much money in those days, so some independent operators set up "wildcat bleachers" just beyond the outfield walls of the ballpark. These were rows of wooden seats, on stilts, along Cherry Street and National Avenue and they cut into the team's slender profits. Seats in the "wildcat bleachers" went for 15¢, though they'd be dropped to as

Wildcat Bleachers in early 1900s.

low as a nickel when the Tigers weren't doing well. The fire marshall finally tore them down as a hazard to the neighborhood.

Twenty men have owned the Tigers over the years, beginning with James D. Burns in 1901. He was the sheriff of Wayne County and a local hotel man. His first manager was George Stallings, who later went on to manage the 1914 "Miracle Braves."

The first American League game ever played in Detroit was on April 25, 1901. The ballpark held a little over 6,000, but 10,023 showed up.

That's a Lot of Hot Dogs

In their 85 years in the American League, the Tigers have played to 85,125,893 fans—or an average of just more than 1,000,000 a year.

Milwaukee took a 7–0 lead and was ahead 13–4 in the ninth inning. The Tigers rallied for 10 runs and pulled out a 14–13 victory.

No kidding, Sparky. That's how it all started.

THE LONGEST DAY

The game started at 1:30 P.M. It ended seven hours later. It was the longest game in the history of baseball.

By far.

The Tigers and Yankees went 22 innings on that memorable Sunday, June 24, 1962. The Yankees finally won 9–7 but not before the 35,638 fans consumed 32,200 hot dogs, 41,000 bottles of beer, and 34,500 bottles of pop.

They played so long that the Michigan labor laws made them shut down the concession stands at 8:15 because women were not permitted to work more than 10 hours on a Sunday.

Matt Dennis, a sportswriter for the *Windsor Star*, got up from his seat in the press box in the 18th inning and announced: "I've got to leave—my visa just expired."

The old record was five hours and nineteen minutes, so the Tigers and Yankees shattered the mark by one hour and forty-one minutes.

The next day the Hall of Fame in Cooperstown called the author of this book, who also happened to be the official scorer of the game, and asked him to send along a copy of the official box score.

They also asked for his picture, his story, and a tape of his voice recounting the unusual incidents of the day.

He figured his place was fixed forever in the lore and legend of baseball.

Until two years later—on May 31, 1964—the New York Mets and San Francisco Giants played a 23-inning game that lasted seven hours and twenty-three minutes and the curators at Cooperstown took—

the author's box score . . .
his story . . .
his picture . . .
his voice . . .

And put them into a small box and stored them in the basement of the Hall of Fame.

It's Opening Day in 1907 and that's Davy Jones waiting for the pitcher to throw a snowball.

Tiger fans, circa 1910. It must have been Derby Day in the ballpark.

THE HOUSE
THE TIGERS BUILT

The overhang. Nobody else in baseball has an overhang like the Tigers.

It is the only place in the game where the upper deck in right field sticks out farther than the lower deck. How many times did Al Kaline stand under the overhang tapping his glove in anticipation of making the catch, only to have the ball come down in the front row of the upper deck?

It's a charming place, Tiger Stadium. You can hit the ball into the lower deck, into the upper deck, off the facing between the two decks, off posts, seats, and foul poles, or off the third deck, the roof, and the light towers. Sometimes you can hit the ball all the way out of sight. Home runs can be great adventures in Tiger Stadium.

One time Rocky Colavito, playing left field, got so mad when the fans laughed at one of his catches that he threw the ball over the right-field roof in anger.

He is the only one ever to clear the roof with his arm.

Ever since they've been in the American League, the Tigers have played at the same site—the corner of Michigan and Trumbull. At first their ballpark was named Bennett Park in honor of their old catcher, Charlie Bennett. The wooden grandstand seated 6,000.

The park was reconstructed and renamed Navin Field and opened in 1912 with concrete and steel stands.

This was the start of the facility that stands to this day.

Originally, Navin Field seated 29,000 and favored right-handed batters. It was only 345 down the left-field line compared to 370 in right. When Walter O. Briggs took over the team from Frank Navin in 1936, he renamed the park Briggs Stadium and expanded to 54,900 seats—including the bleacher section in center field.

John E. Fetzer took the name of Briggs Stadium off the roof and replaced it with Tiger Stadium in 1961. He sold the historic plant to the City of Detroit for $1 in 1977 and leased it back for 30 years with an option for another 30 years.

It was at this point that the old green seats were removed and replaced with blue and orange seats—a slam at a great tradition in Detroit.

The Tigers said they could not get green seats that would reproduce in plastic. A call to the seat manufacturer in Grand Rapids produced a response of, "Hey, I can give them any kind of green they want—sea green, pea green, forest green, grass green . . . they wanted blue and orange, so don't mess up my order by writing about it."

Today, Tiger Stadium seats 52,806 and the best seat in the house is still Jim Campbell's private box down the right-field line. He's got that one-way glass where he can look out and see you but you can't look in and see him.

Alas, not everybody can get in to watch the Tigers.

This is not Cy Young. It is Coleman Young, a right-hander of some repute.

The old announcer, Van Patrick, is breaking in a young announcer by the name of George Kell.

Tigers on Radio

1927-1942: Ty Tyson
1934-1942: Harry Heilman
1943-1950: Harry Heilman (shared broadcast with Van Patrick in 1949)
1951: Ty Tyson-Paul Williams
1952: Van Patrick
1953-1955: Van Patrick-Dizzy Trout
1956-1958: Van Patrick-Mel Ott

1959: Van Patrick-George Kell
1960-1963: George Kell-Ernie Harwell
1964: Ernie Harwell-Bob Scheffing
1965-: Ernie Harwell-Gene Osborn
1967-1972: Ernie Harwell-Ray Lane
1973-1986: Ernie Harwell-Paul Carey

Q. WHO INVENTED THE CHEST PROTECTOR?

A. IT WAS NONE OTHER THAN OUR OLD FRIEND, CHARLIE BENNETT, THE TIGER CATCHER FROM 1885. HE WAS ASHAMED OF IT AT FIRST, THINKING IT MADE HIM LOOK LIKE A SISSY, SO HE TRIED TO HIDE IT UNDER HIS UNIFORM.

THE 17-RUN INNING

It was like a bad dream to pitcher Steve Gromek. He sat in the bullpen in Fenway Park and watched in silence as the Red Sox scored run after run against his new team, the Tigers, until the final score mounted to 17–1.

The date was June 17, 1953.

Gromek thought to himself: "What am I doing here?"

If he thought his first day in a Detroit uniform was bad, he hadn't seen anything yet. He got into the game the next day and the Red Sox scored 17 runs again. This time they did it in one inning.

On June 18, 1953, the Red Sox sent 23 men to plate in the 48-minute carnage. They turned a routine 5–3 game into a crushing 23–3 rout.

"I never saw anything like it," Gromek recalled. "They got some clean hits, but most of them were flukes. The ball kept bouncing just of the reach of our infielders or falling in front of our outfielders."

Gromek was charged with nine of the runs. Gene Stephens got three hits in the inning for the Red Sox.

Gromek was removed from the game by manager Freddie Hutchinson. He figured he'd had it after just one appearance in a Detroit uniform. When Hutchinson approached him in the clubhouse after the game, he was sure of it. He thought he was gone.

All Hutchinson said was: "You're starting when we get to Philadelphia."

Gromek not only started against the Philadelphia A's—he shut them out.

AFTER DARK

In 1985 the Tigers played 106 games at night. Nothing unusual about that, except there was a time in the not too distant past when they played no games at night.

Detroit's first night game was played on June 20, 1939, in Philadelphia. The Tigers blanked Connie Mack's A's 5–0.

It was not until nine years later—on June 15, 1948—that they played their first night game in Detroit. The Tigers were the last of the eight American League teams at the time to install lights. They went up 13 years after the first night game in Cincinnati.

The Tigers, a very conservative organization, had tried twilight games, without lights, starting at 5:00 P.M. But some of these became a fiasco. The players wound up groping around in the semidarkness and some of the games could not be completed. They knew so little about lights that they started their first night game at 9:30 P.M. They thought the lights would not take effect until it was almost totally dark. Detroit was on daylight savings time and so it did not start to get dark until 9:00.

They opened the gates at 6:00 that first night, and the fans started pour-

Tiger Stadium at night . . . or how it looks to Tom Monaghan when he slips into town in his helicopter.

Q. WHAT TWO MOMENTOUS EVENTS TOOK PLACE ON MAY 2, 1939?

A. ONE, THAT WAS THE DAY LOU GEHRIG'S CONSECUTIVE-GAME STREAK OF 2,130 CAME TO AN END IN DETROIT.
TWO, THAT WAS THE DAY GATES BROWN WAS BORN. THE GATER BECAME THE TIGERS' GREATEST PINCH HITTER, COLLECTING 107 PINCH HITS IN HIS CAREER.

The gang lines up early for the 1936 opener.

ing in, buying up 20,000 seats and filling the ballpark to capacity. The Tigers held batting practice from 7:15 until 8:00, then the Philadelphia A's hit from 8:00 until 8:30.

They staged a "control contest" with pitchers on both teams aiming the ball through a paper target set up at home plate. This took a half hour.

Both teams took infield practice, and then for 20 minutes everyone just sat there waiting for the last light to leave the sky.

Finally, at 9:28 P.M. (EDT), the lights came on and the crowd let out

It will be the beginning of the end of major-league baseball.

—Frank Navin, Tiger owner, on night baseball

a spontaneous "Oooooooh!" The A's won the game, beating Hal Newhouser 4–1, but that seemed second-

ary. The blazing lights left everyone bug-eyed.

The next day, Lyall Smith, sports editor of the *Detroit Free Press*, wrote in his column: "For some reason I can't explain, all the action looks faster under the lights. Runners appear to rip down the baselines faster than they do in the afternoon. Every ball that starts out from the bat appears headed for the stands.

"Just what causes such an obvious optical illusion is something for an oculist, psychiatrist or somebody like that to explain. But the game does look faster at night."

The Tigers have now played 3,087 games at night.

FISH STORIES

Home run stories are like fish stories. The more you tell them, the longer they get.

Who can decide who has hit the longest home run of all time? Nobody. But it's fun to try.

It was always felt that the longest home run Detroit ever saw was hit by Babe Ruth in 1926. He hit it off a pitcher named Lil Stoner. This was before they had the double-deck stands in right field and the ball cleared the fence and rolled to the corner of Brooklyn and Cherry streets. It was measured at 626 feet, but that was on a roll. How many

others might have gone as far—or farther if they had not hit some obstruction?

Tape measure home runs are in the eyes of the beholder.

But now here comes a man named Paul E. Susman, who offers evidence that Mickey Mantle—not Babe Ruth—hit the longest home run in Detroit. He says it happened on September 10, 1960, and came off Paul Foytack. It was Mantle's third blast over the right-field roof in Tiger Stadium.

This is Susman's account as printed in *The Baseball Digest*:

The ball went out at the 370 foot mark, through the light tower, deflecting off a pipe, and then disappeared from sight. Hall of Famer George Kell, a Detroit announcer, spontaneously said, "It was the longest ball I ever saw." Veteran announcer and Hall of Famer Ernie Harwell, who had witnessed most of the previous roof shots [as well as Kirk Gibson's 1983 homer], said, "Mantle's blast was about the longest one we've ever seen." Watson Spoelstra, a veteran reporter, confirmed that the ball went through the second tower. Neal Fenkell, a veteran observer dating back to the early 1950s, said, "It was the longest ball of all time, no doubt about it."

Sensing the historic nature of the blast, the late Ed Browalski and Edgar Hayes, Detroit sports reporters, pursued the final landing site. Browalski and Hayes discovered the ball completely cleared Trumbull Avenue (110 feet wide) and descended on the fly into the Brooks Lumber Yard. This information was given to them by a lumberyard worker named Paul Baldwin (now deceased) who was an eyewitness.

Years later I found a lumberyard worker named Sam Cameron, a longtime employee of the Brooks Lumber Yard who had started part-time in 1953 and then switched to full-time in 1959. Paul Baldwin and Sam had worked together for many years and knew each other well. Baldwin showed Sam the precise spot where Mantle's drive landed on a fly.

When I interview Sam, he didn't hesitate an instant as he pinpointed the exact landing site. We measured the depth of the stands, Trumbull Avenue, and the distance to where the ball was seen on a fly. The final measurement came out to 643 feet, making this a new record for precisely measured home run distance, surpassing Mantle's previous 565-foot shot in Washington's Griffith Stadium in 1953. The calculations were done by Bob Schiewie, a mathematical expert.

This is how left field looked before they put up the left-field stands in 1938.

Babe Ruth's epic home run in 1926. It went 626 feet.

That's one home run story.

Here's another.

Back in 1956, Mantle hit another over-the-roof shot—also off Paul Foytack. None of us had ever seen anything like it before. It took one bounce on the roof between the light towers and went out into Trumbull Avenue. It was only the second ball ever hit out of the Detroit ballpark. The first was by Ted Williams in 1939.

We were so astounded to see such a massive blast that we felt, at *The Detroit Times*, it deserved special treatment.

The next day we asked the right-fielder of the Tigers, Al Kaline, to get into a fielding pose and our photographer took a picture of him. Then he took a picture of the right-field roof, where Mantle's home run had gone out the day before.

We took both pictures into our art department and they reduced the size of Kaline to conform with the

Endurance Record

The Tigers have played more games than any other American League team— 13,192.

Unfortunately, they haven't won more games than anyone else. That honor goes to the Yankees with 7,421 victories. The Tigers have won 6,801 times, putting them 620 victories behind.

roof. Then they cut out his picture and pasted it on the front of the roof.

The next day we came out with our version of the "Mantle Shift."

The photo looked so authentic

that John McHale, who was the general manager of the Tigers at the time, called up John Manning, the editor of *The Detroit Times*, and complained to him.

"How dare your men take my

Ed Browalski, the late baseball writer of the *Polish Daily News*, checks out his lineup for a father-and-son game in Tiger Stadium. Miss ya, Big Ed.

Here is the man who broadcast the Tigers for the first time back in 1927, the venerable Ty Tyson. It is after the war and Ty is doing a telecast for WWJ-TV. They didn't have a TV booth in those days but it didn't seem to bother Ty. He seems very interested in what's going on.

Who remembers when the broadcast booth was little bigger than a telephone booth? That's Paul Williams at the mike when he handled the play-by-play for the Tigers in 1951.

The night the press box burned in 1974. "What a shame," said general manager Jim Campbell, "that it happened in the winter when the writers weren't around."

Q. WHAT WAS SO SPECIAL ABOUT THE FIRST AMERICAN LEAGUE GAME EVER PLAYED IN DETROIT?

A. MORRIS GEORGE (DOC) AMOLE OF BUFFALO THREW A NO-HITTER AGAINST THE TIGERS. YOU HAVE TO LOOK HARD FOR IT IN THE RECORD BOOKS SINCE IT TOOK PLACE IN 1900 AND THE AMERICAN LEAGUE DIDN'T GAIN MAJOR-LEAGUE STATUS UNTIL 1901.

rightfielder and put him on the edge of the roof . . . he could have been killed if he'd lost his balance," McHale roared into the phone.

Manning, a gentle sort, didn't know what was going on and tried to placate McHale. He assured McHale that he would talk to his men in the sports department.

Even when we told him it was a hoax, Manning found it difficult to believe. The artists had done a great job with the two photographs. McHale grumbled about it for days. He still thought we had pulled off a fast one.

THE FESTIVAL OF SURPRISES

"Attention please. Batting for Frank Saucier of the Browns, No. 1/8th—Eddie Gaedel."

What's this—a joke? Who's the midget coming out of the St. Louis Browns' dugout swinging half a dozen 10-inch bats?

The fans in Sportsman's Park in St. Louis couldn't believe their eyes. The crowd was going crazy. A midget in the major leagues?

Yep—and the joke was on the Tigers.

Bill Veeck, the old showman himself, promised the folks a few surprises if they came out for the Sunday doubleheader against the Tigers. The date was August 19, 1951.

Veeck, who owned the Browns in those days, billed the day as a "Festival of Surprises," and between the games of the doubleheader he had jugglers, jitterbug dancers, and a ragtime band performing out on the field.

The fans hadn't seen anything yet.

The Browns had lost the first game of the doubleheader and now manager Zack Taylor was at home plate turning in his lineup for the second game to umpire Ed Hurley. He had Saucier leading off and playing right field.

Now, here came this—what? This midget? He was strutting to the plate, all 3½ feet and 50 pounds of him, to bat leadoff for the Browns.

Hurley was stunned.

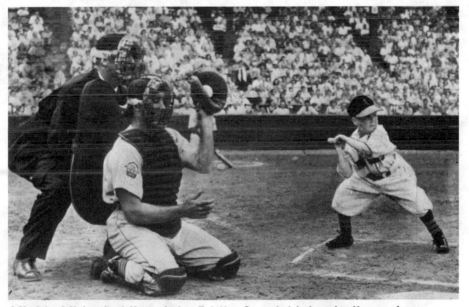

Mighty Midget at the plate. Eddie Gaedel takes ball one from Tiger pitcher Bob Cain. That's Bob Swift behind the plate and umpire Ed Hurley behind him. How come they're all so serious?

No Sense of Humor

For years the sign on the door of the visitor's dressing room in Tiger Stadium read: "Visitor's Clubhouse—No Visitors Allowed."

A newspaperman finally noticed the sign and put it in his story. The next day, the Tigers painted over the sign.

He pulled off his mask and said: "Wait a minute here!" He stormed over to the St. Louis dugout to confront Taylor. Nobody was going to make a mockery of this game, not even the flamboyant Veeck, who was howling in glee from his perch in the press box.

"What's going on?" Hurley boomed.

Taylor quietly handed him two sheets of paper. One was an official American League contract with Gaedel's name on it, the other a letter informing the American League office in Chicago of Gaedel's "acquisition."

Hurley was fuming. He knew he was being had but could do nothing about it. He marched back to the plate and said: "All right, let's go!"

Gaedel stepped into the batter's box and pounded—or patted—his bat on the plate.

Catcher Bob Swift of the Tigers went down on his knees and held his glove up as a target for pitcher Bob Cain. He didn't even give him a sign. Cain shrugged and threw the ball.

Ball one.

The crowd was absolutely hysterical. Cain seemed to be enjoying it all. He made four pitches to Gaedel—all over his head. Gaedel trotted down to first base with a walk and the noise from the stands all but split the afternoon air.

Veeck had pulled of the biggest stunt of his life. Gaedel never played again. The next day he was declared "illegal" by the league office, but the 18,369 fans saw a kind of history they would never forget.

TRIVIA TIME: OK, recite this story of the midget to your friends. Tell it in taverns, on airplanes, in the office, and especially out in the bleachers.

Then ask: "Who did they send in to run for Eddie Gaedel?"

It was Jim Delsing, the outfielder who later played for the Tigers. Be sure to bet a beer on it.

Tigers' Ninth

Most famous inning in Detroit baseball history (October 7, 1935):

Clifton struck out. Cochrane singled off Herman's glove. Gehringer smashed a grounder to Cavarretta, Cochrane reaching second. Goslin singled to center field, scoring Cochrane with the winning run. One run, two hits, no errors, one left.

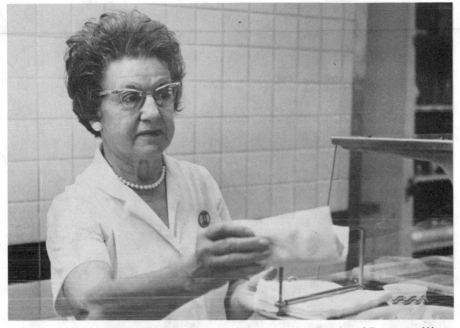

This is our Agnes, who served us in the press box for 25 years. We will never forget her.

Those also serve who watch and wait at midnight.

DETROIT MANAGERS: A STRANGE BREED

Bet you never knew these things about the managers in Detroit:

- *Sparky Anderson*—His favorite breakfast is waffles. He seldom orders anything else.
- *Mayo Smith*—He was known as America's Guest because he free-loaded meals and drinks in both leagues.

Meet Mayo Smith, "America's Guest." He was also the manager of the Tigers when they won it all in 1968.

- *Ty Cobb*—The old firebrand astounded his players in his first year on the job by canceling morning workouts in spring training and telling everyone to sleep until noon if they wanted.
- *Red Rolfe*—He was so weak from colitis that he had to sit on cushions in the dugout.
- *Charlie Dressen*—He once baked a cherry cobbler without any cherries for the writers.

- *Bill Armour*—His wife was so caught up in the game that he had to go to her box seat and ask her which pitchers to use.
- *Joe Gordon*—He claimed he played his entire career without using an athletic supporter.
- *Bill Norman*—He would drink beer two at a time and knock off a half dozen within a half hour after every game.
- *Bob Scheffing*—While working with Ernie Harwell on the radio, he went on the air one night in Boston and said: "Hi, this is Ernie Harwell along with Bob Scheffing. . . ."
- *Jack Tighe*—He once told a rookie player when the Tigers trained next to Lodwick Air Force Base: "If anyone asks you to go on the runway for a ball, don't do it. It means they're after your job."
- *Bucky Harris*—Whenever he was asked a tough question by a reporter, he simply let out a whistle and nobody knew how to quote a whistle.
- *Fred Hutchinson*—He was offered the job after the Tigers tried to give it to Schoolboy Rowe, who was out fishing and missed the call from owner Spike Briggs.
- *Steve O'Neill*—He found out he was fired while cutting the grass at his home in Cleveland.
- *Mickey Cochrane*—After he was beaned by Bump Hadley of the Yankees, his wife visited him in the hospital and asked if she could get him anything. Cochrane replied: "Yeah, a new head."
- *Hughie Jennings*—He once ordered Claude Rossman to lay down a bunt, but when Rossman crossed him up and hit a home run, Jennings fined him $50.

Herbie Redmond, your friendly groundskeeper, saying "Hell-ooooooo, Detroit!"

TIGER KIDS

William Brown—son of Gates—
waits his turn in the on-deck
circle.

Aurelio Rodriguez, Jr.—son of
Aurelio Rodriguez, Sr.—thinks
it's lunchtime.

John Wockenfuss, Jr.—son of John Wockenfuss, Sr.—
gets ready to step up with the bases loaded.

Brian Wilcox—son of Milt Wilcox—fields makes a bare-handed stop of a vicious grounder and starts a triple play.

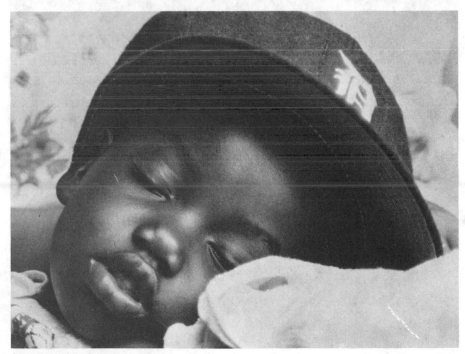

Seventh inning . . . zzzzzzz.

BASEBALL TALK

They used to serve drinks in the press box at old Briggs Stadium. This was when Spike Briggs ran the team. He liked to have a little pop during the games and he had a bar set up in the back room.

Lloyd Northard of the UPI got himself a drink one day while watching a game. He put it at his desk. A foul ball came screaming back into the press box and hit Northard's glass. It sheared off the top of the glass in a smooth circle and didn't spill a drop of the drink.

"Last one to the roof is a rotten egg."

The ladies line up for Ladies Day in 1932.

Signs of the times.

PART II
OLD ENGLISH "D"

TIGERS FROM A TO Z

- *Aber, Al*—The only one who got Ted Williams out on that memorable 8-for-9 tear in 1954 and demanded immediate enshrinement in Cooperstown.
- *Aguirre, Hank*—The pitcher who once went 2-for-80 and won the MHH Award (Most Horrible Hitter): a drugstore bat with six holes drilled in it.
- *Amoros, Sandy*—The old Brooklyn outfielder who told everyone his name sounded like "love on the beach."
- *Bertoia, Reno*—The rookie third baseman from Windsor, Ontario, whose mother packed him a bag of meatball sandwiches on his first road trip because she didn't think the team would feed him right.
- *Bilko, Steve*—The massive first baseman who would stuff towels under the door and around the windows and take a "steamer" by turning on all the hot water faucets in the bathroom.
- *Boone, Ray*—The hard-hitting third baseman of the fifties who once hit seven home runs in one season off Arnold Portocarrero of the Philadelphia A's. Nobody could understand how one batter could hit one pitcher so consistently, until Boone explained: "When he went into his windup, if I could see the *A* on his cap, I knew it was a fastball. If I couldn't, I knew it was a curve." He revealed his secret after Portocarrero left the game. Booney swung only at the fast balls.

- *Boros, Steve*—The third baseman from Flint who had weak ankles and would sit in front of his locker before the games and work his feet around in a box of mud.
- *Boswell, Dave*—The right-handed pitcher who got into a fist fight with manager Billy Martin in an alley outside of a Detroit bar and when he was beaten up said: "He was the pitcher and I was the catcher."
- *Brady, Jim*—The kid from Notre Dame who pitched in the annual Hall of Fame game in Cooperstown in 1956 with a stray dog wandering out on the field and playing short center field behind him.
- *Brideweser, Jim*—The laconic infielder who was known as "Dead Body" among the writers in Detroit.
- *Bridges, Rocky*—The smooth-fielding shortstop who used to get to the ballpark at 10 o'clock in the morning with Eddie Yost and sit around and spit tobacco juice into a bucket because there was nothing to do around the hotel and he had to think of some way to kill all the time before night games.
- *Brinkman, Eddie*—The shortstop who finally made a name for himself when he was asked on a Detroit TV station what he thought of the division-winning Tigers in 1972 and replied *on the air*: "This is one good bleeping team."

Aurelio Rodriguez (right) breaks up at Eddie Brinkman's "colorful comment" about the 1972 Tigers.

- *Brown, Dick*—The quiet catcher who died of cancer at age 35, never once complaining about his condition.
- *Brown, Gates*—The pinch-hitting outfielder who went to a banquet with Willie Horton and, when asked what Horton took in high school, said: "Willie took algebra, history, English, and overcoats."
- *Brown, Ike*—The happy-go-lucky guy who loved his life in baseball. He told everyone: "I'm the Tigers' DS—designated sitter."
- *Bruton, Billy*—The skinny-legged outfielder who retired in 1964 at the age of 36 and told everyone at the press conference he was really 39—"I kind of cheated three years on you guys," grinned Billy B.
- *Bunning, Jim*—"The Lizard," who was one of the greatest strikeout pitchers in baseball history, but don't ask him how many times he ever fanned Nellie Fox of the White Sox. Answer: 0.
- *Burnside, Pete*—The skinny lefthanded pitcher who used to run for a whole hour after practice while his manager, Jimmie Dykes, would shake his head and say: "If you could win games with your legs, this guy would be a 30-game winner."
- *Cash, Norm*—The slugging first baseman who got so disgusted when Nolan Ryan was pitching a no-hitter against the Tigers in 1973 that he dragged a chair leg to home plate and told the umpire: "I may as well try to hit him with this thing."
- *Castillo, Marty*—The quick-talking catcher and third baseman who fell into such a batting slump in 1985 that he said: "They're going to have to hold a 'Live Aid' concert just for me."
- *Chrisley, Neil*—The little-known outfielder who sat in front of the clubhouse in Lakeland and asked: "Anyone know the record for ofurs?" A writer asked: "Ofurs?" "Sure," said Chrisley, "You know—0 fur 10, 0 fur 20, 0 fur 30. . . ."
- *Cicotte, Eddie*—The old pitcher from the Chicago Black Sox scandal who, in the waning days of his life, sat on the porch of his home in Livonia, Michigan, pulled up his pant legs, pointed to his feet and said: "See what I'm wearing—white socks."
- *Colavito, Rocky*—The home run-hitting outfielder who got mad at a certain baseball writer and stayed mad at him for years, all because the guy wrote: "The Tigers are putting Colavito into left field, because he has the feet for it."
- *Comer, Wayne*—The reserve outfielder who was feeling pretty good that day manager Mayo Smith called him into his office and told him: "Wayne, you're going to hit .295 this season." Just as Comer started to smile, his manager added: "But it's going to be in Montgomery."
- *Doby, Larry*—The veteran outfielder who hit a ball into the seats in batting practice on the day before the 1959 season, prompting *The Detroit News* to run an eight-column banner headline on page one: "Doby in Home Run

Rob Falls, age 11, interviews Rocky Colavito, Jr., in the 1962 season. Somebody had to find out what was going on in the Colavito clan since Rocky Sr. wasn't talking to a certain baseball writer. All the writer did was print Colavito's RNBIs— runs *not* batted in.

Form." He played 18 games for the Tigers, never hit one in a game, and was sold to the White Sox a month into the season.

- *Evans, Darrell*—A quiet man who applauds himself after hitting a home run.
- *Federoff, Al*—The utility infielder whose addition to the team was questioned in an interview with manager Red Rolfe, who replied: "Yes, I think we'll be better off with Federoff."
- *Fernandez, Chico*—The moody infielder who was acquired from the Phillies, prompting one writer to say: "The Tigers will try to solve their shortstop problem with a problem shortstop."
- *Foytack, Paul*—The happy-go-lucky pitcher who, when asked for his reaction about the Tigers' screening in the lower deck in right field to cut down on home runs, said: "Great! What about the upper deck?"
- *Garver, Ned*—The veteran pitcher whose trick knee used to pop out of place, and he would sit on the mound while the trainer came out with a mallet and popped it back into place.

- *Groth, Johnny*—The man who lived in Chicago with his wife and five daughters but, whenever the Tigers played in Chicago, would stay at the team's hotel instead of going home because "a guy's got to get his rest."
- *Horton, Willie*—The slugging outfielder who hit a towering foul ball over home plate in Fenway Park, which smacked a pigeon in flight and sent it plummeting to the ground, where it fell dead on home plate.
- *Host, Gene*—The seldom-used relief pitcher who said he felt good about his career because Nap Ross told him he'd make it in the major leagues and, when asked who Nap Ross was, replied: "I don't know."
- *Ivie, Mike*—The first baseman who inspired arguments about whether he looked more like Sonny Tufts or Aldo Ray, the beefcake movie actors, and who had a psychological hang-up about throwing the ball to his teammates.
- *Jones, Sam*—The pitcher who would chomp on a toothpick and glare when asked a question.
- *Kell, George*—The veteran third baseman who made two of the three outs for the Red Sox on the day in 1953 when they scored 17 runs in one inning against the Tigers.
- *Lund, Don*—The leftfielder for the Tigers during the 17-run inning who, when asked what he remembered about it, said: "Nothing. I can't remember a single run scoring."
- *Maas, Duke*—"The Duke of Utica," so named because he seemed to have it all—a handsome face, a blazing fastball, and a beauty-queen wife. He suddenly fell ill and died, and everything turned to ashes.
- *Martin, John*—The little-known pitcher who spent just one season in Detroit and was so quiet that nobody ever heard him speak a word, including "Please pass the salt."
- *Masterson, Walt*—The veteran pitcher who came over from Washington and wore dark glasses and never smiled and looked like the meanest man in the world.
- *Mathews, Eddie*—The Hall of Fame third baseman from Milwaukee who allegedly was a steadying influence in the clubhouse when the Tigers won it all in 1968. The thing that sticks in your mind, however, is the way he bumped into a photographer on the field as he was chasing a foul fly and threw the ball at him.
- *Maxwell, Charlie*—"Old Paw Paw," who loved to needle the sportswriters by saying, "Yup, I worked for a triweekly back home in Paw Paw—we tried to put it out weekly."
- *McLain, Denny*—The blond hurler who showed up as a redhead one day and said: "Aw, whattaya talkin' about? I've always been a redhead."
- *Mossi, Don*—A not-so-handsome man, with that long nose, a dark beard, and those large ears, but the kids loved him as if he were Prince Valiant and he got a little better looking every time he stopped and gave a young fan a few minutes of his time.

- *Nieman, Bob*—The outfielder who wasn't very good in the field and always called himself "Bob Nieman and his golden glove."
- *Oana, Prince*—The man with the strange name who hit a line drive over second base, and the ball kept rising and rising until it crashed into the center-field seats. Mel Allen, on the Yankee broadcast, called it one of the most remarkable home runs he'd ever seen—a 420-foot line drive that never got more than 20 feet off the ground.
- *Osborne, Bobo*—The hulking left-handed slugger, brought up from Charleston, who said he was going to demolish the right-field stands and hit all of five home runs in five years with the Tigers.
- *Oyler, Ray*—The slick-fielding shortstop who would get a dark, hurtful look in his eyes when everybody around him was celebrating one more victory in 1968. He was having trouble hitting the ball back to the pitcher.
- *Papi, Stan*—The light-hitting utility player who asked the newspapers not to print his salary because it was so small that he was ashamed of it.
- *Phillips, Bubba*—The leftfielder who laughed the day they wrote he played left field as if he were wearing roller skates. "Not a bad idea," he said. "I might get myself a pair."
- *Porter, J. W.*—The freckle-faced catcher who was brought up on a paternity charge. He liked to write poetry in his spare time, and when the paternity case went to court, sports editor Don Wolfe of the *Toledo Blade* wrote: "While the other players are down in the lobby, Porter is in his room, practicing his hobby."
- *Quelich, George*—The only "Q" the Tigers ever had, who played only one season—1931. When he was asked for his autograph, he said: "Why would anyone want my name on a piece of paper?"
- *Rakow, Ed*—The righthanded pitcher whose big claim to fame was that he played quarterback for the Bloomfield Rams, a semipro team in Pennsylvania. He was a big star until a slope-shouldered, sallow, hollow-chested guy came along and took his job. Rakow will never forget Johnny Unitas.
- *Regan, Phil*—One of the nicest men who ever pitched in Detroit. So why was he called "the Vulture" when he went over to the National League? Just because he spit on the ball?
- *Rogovin, Saul*—Half of the answer to baseball nut Bert Gordon's favorite trivia question: "Name the only all-Jewish battery in the history of the Tigers." The other half of the answer is Joe Ginsberg.
- *Rozema, Dave*—The flaky pitcher who was seen washing his car outside his motel in Lakeland, using Brillo pads to get it cleaner.
- *Samford, Ron*—The light-hitting shortstop who created baseball history when he dropped his bat while swinging at one of Hoyt Wilhelm's knuckleballs but went through his swing anyway. He said he was trying to "fist the ball into left field."
- *Sharon, Dick*—The reserve outfielder who opened his fan mail one day to find a request for six of his autographs because that's how many the letter writer needed to get one of Bill Freehan.

No, Dave Rozema isn't telling pitching coach Roger Craig how tall he'd like to be when he grows up. Rozie wasn't *that* flaky.

- *Staub, Rusty*—The fusspot who insisted on a clause in his contract stipulating that the airport runways had to be a certain length before he'd get on any of the planes with the Tigers.
- *Tobik, Dave*—The struggling relief pitcher whose sportswriter wife lasted longer in the major leagues than he did.
- *Ujdur, Jerry*—The grim-faced pitcher whose short stint with the Tigers was a blessing because it was so easy to misspell his name "Jerry Udjur."
- *Valentinetti, Vito*—The portly pitcher who was known as the "Maître d' " because he looked like one.

- *Wert, Don*—The smooth-fielding third baseman who played eight years in Detroit and never raised his voice above a whisper.
- *Wertz, Vic*—The hard-hitting outfielder and first baseman who walked clear across the field from the dugout of the St. Louis Browns to extend his hand to a brand-new baseball writer on the beat, saying: "Hi, I'm Vic Wertz . . . glad to see you traveling with the Tigers."
- *Yewcic, Tom*—The Michigan State quarterback who tried to make it as a catcher but got his sports mixed up and tried to knock down the backstop with a slide into homeplate.
- *Zernial, Gus*—"Ozark Ike," so called because he would eat airplane steaks, four or five at a time, popping them into his mouth like after-dinner mints.

I'm pretty good at digging graves. In 10 years, no one's ever dug himself out of one yet.

—Richie Hebner

Ty Cobb was a diabetic.

Sister Ballparks

Tiger Stadium and Boston's Fenway Park are two of baseball's most revered ballparks, but they have even more in common. They opened their doors on the same day— April 20, 1912, with the Tigers beating Cleveland 6–5 and Boston beating the Yankees 7–6 in 11 innings.

The Battalion of Death

The infield in 1934 was composed of Hank Greenberg at first, Charlie Gehringer at second, Billy Rogell at short, and Marv Owen at third.

They were dubbed the "Battalion of Death."

Every man played every game that season except Hank Greenberg, who missed only one. He sat out Yom Kippur.

You know what's wrong with your team? You don't hit enough double-baggers.

—Harry Sisson, former treasurer, to manager Jack Tighe

THE BIRD

You could never get near Mark Fidrych's locker. Cakes and flowers and presents and boxes of mail were stacked around his locker. You had to climb over them to get close to him.

They all loved the Bird.

They loved him more than any athlete they had ever had in Detroit, and how long did he last? One fleeting summer, that's all.

For four months—June, July, August, and September of 1976—he flashed across our sky. He won nineteen games and lost only nine and that wasn't a bad record for a kid with not much of a background in the minor leagues.

Hardly anybody talked about his won-lost record, though.

They talked about his style.

His spirit. His enthusiasm.

The way he talked to the ball.

Nobody ever had it like this young man in the summer of 1976, and to this day the mere mention of his name brings a smile to the faces of baseball fans in Detroit.

Also a look of sadness . . . because that's all he had and it's all we had: four precious months.

The next spring—1977—Mark Fidrych hurt his knee, then his shoulder, and was never the same again. His Camelot—our Camelot—lasted four months.

I don't want to be a star. Stars get blamed too much.
—Enos Cabell

Consecutive Games Played by Tigers

Charlie Gehringer—*511*
Charlie Gehringer—*504*
Rocky Colavito—*458*
Ed Brinkman—*434*

(The major-league record is 2,130, by Lou Gehrig of the Yankees.)

Life is nothing but a joy for Mark Fidrych in 1976.

"Come on, ball—stay low. Stay low, ball."

What a wild time it was. They lined up around the block to buy tickets to see him pitch. Every appearance was a "happening," almost a religious experience.

What was he doing?

He was smoothing out the mound, talking to the ball—"Come on, ball, stay low, stay low"—and keeping it low and on the outside. But he did it with great flair and flourish. He turned on a whole town when a whole town needed to be turned on.

Mark Fidrych came into a deprived situation (Detroit was in another of its many economic crises, with the automotive industry under siege from the Japanese car

"Maybe if I smooth out these few pebbles. . . ."

builders), and he made everyone feel good.

He gave them joy.

He gave them pleasure.

He gave them a reason to forget their troubles.

His base pay was $16,000. He earned millions for the Tigers. He became the single greatest attraction this baseball team has ever known—greater, even, than Denny McLain in the year he won his 31 games.

Nobody had ever seen anything like the Bird.

It all ended in the spring of 1977, when he returned to the Tigers and in trying to let the world know he was still around—"Hey, world, this is me, Mark Fidrych, I'm still here"—he jumped up for a fly ball in the outfield and came down on his knee, which twisted under him, and he fell to the ground. He was never the same, even though a whole town hoped and prayed for his recovery.

It is a sad story, but it is also a glad story.

Mark Fidrych is now 31 years old, and he has his farm in Massachusetts, his precious plot of ground, his horses and his pigs, and he is more at ease than he has ever been.

"I have no complaints," he says. "I had more than I ever expected. I did my best and that's all anyone can do. People were good to me and what more could I ask?"

Have a happy life, Mark.

Who's Superstitious?

Bill Armour was manager of the Tigers in 1905 and 1906. He was very jittery. Whenever he saw a butterfly on the field, he made them stop the game and have his players kill it.

━━━━━ BASEBALL TALK ━━━━━

These multimillion-dollar contracts blow Hank Aguirre's mind. He remembers the day in 1965 when he stood before Jim Campbell's desk and the general manager of the Tigers told him he was going to pay him exactly the same salary as the previous year.

Aguirre was furious. He gave Campbell a piece of his mind and started out of his office.

He paused at the door.

"OK, I'll make you a deal," said Aguirre. "I'll sign the contract, but you've got to give me a raise. Make it a penny more than last year and I'm in."

"You're on," said Campbell.

It was the smallest—and quietest—raise in the history of baseball.

What's one home run? If you hit one, they are just going to want you to hit two.

—Mick Kelleher,
who never hit a
major-league
home run

Boots Poffenberger, the eccentric pitcher from the 1930s, loved to sleep late and then order up the "Breakfast of Champions": two fried eggs and a bottle of beer.

Tiger Stolen Bases

Ty Cobb—*865*
Donie Bush—*400*
Sam Crawford—*317*
Ron LeFlore—*294*
George Moriarty—*190*
Bobby Veach—*189*
Charlie Gehringer—*182*
Davy Jones—*140*
Al Kaline—*137*
Gee Walker—*132*
Alan Trammell—*124*

Mike Ivie is a forty-million-dollar airport with a three-dollar control tower.
—Rick Monday

The Tigers' "Rubber Man," Harry Davis, 1932.

Nicknames of Former Tigers

"Hooks" Dauss
"Snooks" Dowd
"Piano Legs" Hickman
"Baby Doll" Jacobson
"Razor" Ledbetter
"Baldy" Louden
"Slim" Love
"Soldier Boy" Murphy
"Stubby" Overmire
"Muddy" Ruel
"Hack" Simmons
"Phenomenal" Smith
"Tubby" Spencer
"Sailor" Stroud
"Icehouse" Wilson
"Mutt" Wilson
"Squanto" Wilson

Tigers' Longest Hitting Streaks

40—Ty Cobb, 1911
35—Ty Cobb, 1917
34—Jonathan Stone, 1930
30—Goose Goslin, 1934
30—Ron LeFlore, 1976

A ball bat is a wondrous weapon.

—Ty Cobb

Q. WHO WAS THE WORST-HITTING PITCHER IN DETROIT HISTORY?

A. NOPE, IT WASN'T HANK AGUIRRE. NOT EVEN CLOSE. FRED GLADDING, A RELIEF PITCHER FROM 1961 TO 1967, WENT TO THE PLATE 40 TIMES AND NEVER GOT A HIT. HE WAS 1 FOR 70 IN THE NATIONAL LEAGUE AND WOUND UP WITH A LIFETIME MARK OF .016.

Paul Richards, who caught for the Tigers in 1943-46, was never fooled by the sportswriters. That's because he was one back home in Texas, writing a column for the Waxahachie paper.

They shouldn't throw at me. I'm the father of five or six kids.

—The immortal
Tito Fuentes

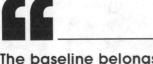

The baseline belongs to me.
—Ty Cobb

Ty Cobb pitched three times for the Tigers—twice in 1918 and once in 1925. He worked a total of five innings, allowing six hits, and was credited with saving one game.

Tigers Hitting Home Runs First Time Up in the Majors

Hack Miller, 1944, at Cleveland
George Vico, 1948, at Chicago
Gates Brown, 1963, at Boston
Bill Roman, 1964, at New York
Gene Lamont, 1970, at Boston
Reggie Sanders, 1974, vs. Oakland at Detroit

The All-Stars of 1937. Left to right: Lou Gehrig, Joe Cronin, Bill Dickey, Joe DiMaggio, Tiger Charlie Gehringer, Jimmie Fox, Tiger Hank Greenberg.

Item: Ty Cobb was paid $1,500 in his first year with the Tigers.

I didn't try too hard. I was afraid I'd get emotionally involved with the cow.

> —Rocky Bridges, after finishing second in a pregame cow-milking contest

The Home Run That Never Was

A moment of silence for Francis Sigafoos, who played 14 games for the Tigers in 1929.

He smacked a ball into the left-field seats, but the umpires made him come back and do it again because they said the pitcher had committed a balk before throwing the ball.

The home run was wiped out and Sigafoos never hit another one.

BASEBALL TALK

Rick Ferrell, nearing 80, remembers what it was like to be a rookie. The longtime scout of the Tigers remembers his first year in the league. It was 1929. He was with the St. Louis Browns.

He was making his first trip into New York City and didn't want anyone to know he was a rookie. When the train pulled into Grand Central Station he decided he would pick out one of the veterans and do what he did. That way he would get to the hotel without drawing any attention to himself.

He selected Lu Blue, the veteran first baseman.

Blue got off the train. Ferrell got off the train. Blue picked up his bag on the platform. Ferrell picked up his bag on the platform. Blue started walking away. Ferrell started walking away.

Blue went down a flight of stairs. Ferrell went down a flight of stairs. Blue noticed Ferrell following him.

"What are you doing?" he asked.

"I'm following you," said Ferrell.

"That's fine," said Blue, ". . . but I'm on my way to my home in New Rochelle."

Sluggers of '61: Rocky Colavito (45 homers, 140 RBIs), Al Kaline (116 runs scored, .324 batting average), and Norm Cash (41 homers, 132 RBIs, .361 batting average). No wonder they're smiling.

TIGERS IN BASEBALL HALL OF FAME

	Pos.	Year Selected	Years at Detroit
Averill, Earl	of	1975	1939–40
Barrow, Edward G.	mgr	1953	1903–04
Brouthers, Dan	1b	1945	1886–88
Cobb, Ty	of-mgr	1936	1905–26
Cochrane, Mickey	c-mgr	1947	1934–38
Crawford, Sam	of	1957	1903–17
Evans, Billy	gen mgr	1973	1947–51
Ferrell, Rick	gen mgr/scout	1984	1950–
Gehringer, Charlie	if	1949	1924–42
Goslin, Goose	of	1968	1934–37
Greenberg, Hank	1b-of	1956	1930–46
Harwell, Ernie	broadcaster	1981	1960–
Harris, Bucky	if-mgr	1975	1929–33 1955–56
Heilman, Harry	of-1b	1952	1914–29
Hoyt, Waite	p	1969	1930–31
Jennings, Hughie	ss-mgr	1945	1907–20
Kaline, Al	of	1980	1953–74
Kell, George	if	1983	1946–52
Manush, Heinie	of	1964	1923–27
Mathews, Eddie	3b-1b	1978	1967–68
Simmons, Al	of	1953	1936
Thompson, Sam	of	1974	1885–88 1906

══ BASEBALL TALK ══

Wally Moses, the friendly old coach, loved to tell about the greatest ovation he ever heard in his life.

It happened near the end of his career. As he was stepping into the plate at Yankee Stadium, the fans stood up and gave out a rousing cheer.

It wasn't for Wally.

The guy on the public address microphone had just said: "Ladies and gentlemen, your attention please. Benito Mussolini, the Italian dictator, has just been put to death in Italy by execution."

SPARKY, SPARKY, AND MORE SPARKY

"Don't tell anyone but this is our hit-and-run sign."

"I wonder if I locked the keys in the car?"

"If we can do this against the Dodgers in the World Series, I'll even stick my tongue out at Tommy Lasorda."

"No comments about my nose, please."

Carol Anderson: the
manager's manager.

"Come on, ump . . . who's
making a joke of this game?"

Charlie Gehringer is in a rut. He hits .350 on Opening Day and stays there all season.

—Lefty Gomez,
Yankee pitcher

Tigers Hitting for Cycle (single, double, triple, and homer in same game)

Bobby Veach, *1920*
Bob Fothergill, *1926*
Gee Walker, *1937*
Charlie Gehringer, *1939*
Vic Wertz, *1947*
George Kell, *1950*
Hoot Evers, *1950*

Q. DID TY COBB EVER SUFFER A SLUMP?

A. YEP, HE ONCE WENT 0 FOR 32. (HE DIDN'T LIKE TO TALK ABOUT IT.)

LAST TIME THEY DID IT

- *Inside-the-park home run:* Kirk Gibson vs. Toronto, October 2, 1985 (Stieb pitching)
- *Home run over roof:* Lou Whitaker vs. Texas, May 13, 1985 (Hooten pitching)
- *Grand-slam home run:* Darrell Evans vs. Milwaukee, August 4, 1985 (Gibson pitching)
- *Back-to-back homers:* Evans and Gibson vs. Toronto, October 2, 1985 (Stieb pitching)
- *Steal of home:* Lance Parrish vs. Boston, July 27, 1984 (Hurst pitching)
- *Hitting for cycle:* Hoot Evers vs. Cleveland, September 7, 1950
- *Three consecutive homers:* Al Kaline, Bill Freehan, and Mickey Stanley at Cleveland, July 29, 1974
- *No-hitter:* Jack Morris at Chicago, April 7, 1984
- *Triple play:* Tom Brookens to Whitaker to Richie Hebner at Milwaukee, August 20, 1980 (Bando batting)

YOU CAN WIN A BET WITH THIS ONE ALMOST EVERY TIME:

Q. NAME THE ONLY TIGER MANAGER WHO NEVER MANAGED THE TIGERS.

A. IT WAS A MAN NAMED WIN MERCER. HE WAS A PITCHER AND WAS NAMED TO MANAGE THE TEAM IN 1903, BUT HE COMMITTED SUICIDE IN SAN FRANCISCO BEFORE EVER GOING TO SPRING TRAINING.

Gehringer and Greenberg retire their numbers in 1983.

Q. EVERYBODY KNOWS THAT CHARLIE MAXWELL, THE CELEBRATED SUNDAY SLUGGER, HAILS FROM PAW PAW, MICHIGAN. BUT WHO WAS THE FIRST PROMINENT PLAYER TO COME OUT OF THAT QUAINT MICHIGAN TOWN?

A. IT WAS BILL KILLEFER, WHO PITCHED BRIEFLY FOR THE TIGERS IN 1907–09. NOBODY KNOWS IF HE HIT ANY ON SUNDAY.

BASEBALL TALK

Al Kaline was having breakfast in the dining room of his hotel in Lakeland when Aurelio Rodriguez approached his table.

"Can I talk to you?" asked Rodriguez.

"Sure," said Kaline. "Sit down."

Rodriguez pulled up a chair. "Tell me," he said, "you retired from baseball?"

Kaline looked at him. "Yes," he said, "I'm retired."

"No more play?" asked Rodriguez.

"No more play," said Kaline.

"You sure?" asked Rodriguez.

"Sure, I'm sure," said Kaline.

"OK," said Rodriguez brightly, "then let me have your swing."

Q. WHO WAS THE ALL-TIME HOLDOUT?

A. IT WAS PITCHER RUFE GENTRY. WHEN THE TIGERS REFUSED TO GRANT HIM A THOUSAND-DOLLAR RAISE IN 1945, HE SPENT THE ENTIRE SEASON AT HIS HOME IN DAISY STATION, NORTH CAROLINA.
THE TIGERS WON THE WORLD SERIES THAT YEAR.

"

I hate Forest Lawn. It's the absolute worst. Those guys dig in tuxedos.

— Richie Hebner,
the celebrated
grave digger

Nobody could ever understand why, when Ty Cobb got on first base, he would stand off in foul territory and kick the bag with his foot.

Cobb never told anyone.

He was trying to move the bag a few inches closer to second.

THE GEORGIA PEACH

Ty Cobb was many things in his life. He was one of the cheapest men ever to play the game of baseball.

In the old days, they had a tradition in Detroit that the men would wear their straw hats to the Labor Day game and the first time the Tigers did anything at all, they would stand up and sail their hats out onto the field. It was a gesture symbolizing the end of summer.

Cobb loved this day. He waited for it every year.

No sooner did the hats come sailing out of the stands than he had the groundskeepers hustling out on the field to pick them up. He had them put the hats into his car and he would take them home with him to be placed on the heads of the donkeys that worked on his farm in Georgia.

"That's nothing," recalled Hank Greenberg. "They say he used to wait until the players were finished showering each day and pick up the small bars of soap off the shower room floor."

This was the same man who became a millionaire many times over through the purchase of Coca-Cola and General Motors stock.

He would give out stock market tips that would result in thousands

Ty Cobb, a big favorite at the 1958 Oldtimers Game.

> I love my father's six graveyards back home. I can't give you the names because they're all Jewish and you couldn't spell them anyway. They're great places to dig, except when it gets cold. Then you've got to chip away at the ice. But a good designated digger can always get the job done.
>
> —Richie Hebner,
> the celebrated
> grave digger

of dollars of profit, then tip the waitress 5¢ at dinner.

It was easy to understand why people despised this man.

He was consumed by the game of baseball. If he couldn't beat you with his body, he'd try to beat you with his brain. He was a left-handed batter who had no set batting stance. He would bat in front of the batter's box or from the rear. He'd swing off his toes or from the back of his heels. He'd swing soft or hard or miss the ball intentionally in order to lull the enemy defenses. Then he'd drop down a bunt and catch everyone flat-footed.

Or he might fake a bunt and send a line drive whistling past their heads. He was a great competitor and an ornery cuss. Few liked Ty Cobb, but all respected him.

Where Babe Ruth was pleasing to the eye, Cobb was pleasing to the mind. He often stole second, third, and home on consecutive plays. Once he did it on three straight pitches. And he always bragged about what he was doing. He was always playing psychological games with his opponents.

He often acted as if he were hurt, but these were ruses to fool the opponent. At the right moment, he would take off and steal a base to win a game. He was a master showman and had to keep thinking of ways to satisfy his ego. Once, during batting practice in Philadelphia, he called where every ball would land, including a line drive into the Yankee dugout that scattered players like pigeons in the park.

An Auspicious Beginning

John P. Sullivan will never forget his major-league debut with the Tigers.

He was a rookie catcher and he was getting the Opening-Night assignment in Kansas City in 1963. As he stood at the plate, taking the last of the warm-up throws from his pitcher . . . spla-a-a-a-a-t! He was pelted by pigeon poop. The umps had to hold up the game and clean him off with a towel.

Our 1924 Tigers with manager Ty Cobb in the middle of the second row.

It was amazing the way he could call his own shots, too. In a game against Boston, a photographer by the name of Dick Sears was dispatched to the ballpark with instructions to "come back with a good action photo." The game was nearly over when Cobb noticed a look of distress on the photographer's face.

"What's the matter?" he asked.

"I'm in trouble," said the photographer. "I've got to get an action shot or my boss is going to give it to me."

Cobb was standing at first base. He told the photographer to go over to third base. Then he flashed a signal to George Moriarty, who was the batter. He gave him the hit-and-run sign. Moriarty reached out and hit the ball behind Cobb for a single into right field. Cobb flew around second and, with spikes flashing,

Mark the date down: July 3, 1906.

That was the day Germany Schaefer made history for the Tigers. That was the day he played one inning in a raincoat against the Cleveland Indians.

Ray Oyler was known as a good-field, no-hit shortstop with the Tigers.

But this was ridiculous: teammate Dick McAuliffe was so sure Oyler was going to make the final out of the inning that he went up to the on-deck circle carrying a glove instead of a bat.

went hard and high into third base, upsetting the Boston third baseman. The photographer got his picture.

Cobb searched for every edge.

For instance, he didn't like to eat too soon after the games. He was too wound up. He felt it was better to return to his hotel and buy a newspaper and stretch out and read for a little while. Sometimes he'd just look out the window or take a nap. Only later in the evening would he go downstairs for dinner. He felt he had to relax for several hours after a game in order for his food to digest properly.

It was the era of "streakers," and Bill Slayback, a young pitcher, was asked what he would do if he were on the mound and a naked girl ran on the field.

He said: "Well, I wouldn't make the next pitch."

His accomplishments were awesome. He won 12 American League batting championships in a 13-year period. When he retired, he had played in more games (3,033), gotten more hits (4,191), scored more runs (2,244), and batted higher (.367) than any player in history. At one time, he held 90 records and he compiled these as a man of average dimensions—6'1" and 175. It's probably a good thing he wasn't around to see Pete Rose break his base hit record. He might have challenged him to a fight at home plate.

Willie Horton was one of the strongest men ever to play for the Tigers.

One day he broke his bat without hitting the ball. Willie tried to check his swing but the top half of the bat broke off, leaving him holding the handle.

Only once could anyone ever remember Cobb's ego getting in his way at the ballpark. This was when he was starting out in the Sally League in 1905. Young Ty, pleased with himself and the world around him, stood in center field and was throwing popcorn into the air and catching it in his mouth. A fly ball came his way and he never saw it. It got past him and cost his pitcher, Eddie Cicotte, a shutout. It was the last time Cobb ever took anything lightly on the field.

Cobb fought death like few men

in history. When he entered Emory Hospital in Atlanta, he brought $1 million in negotiable bonds with him. He arranged them neatly on his nightstand and weighed them down with a pistol.

Ty Cobb died on July 17, 1961, at the age of 74. He was entombed in the family mausoleum in Royston, Georgia. Only two players showed up at his funeral—Mickey Cochrane and Ray Schalk.

Our old friend Cesar Gutierrez, who could beat a mean base fiddle. He also beat out seven hits in seven times at bat in a game against Cleveland.

Willie Hernandez, the man who got more hugs than Wayne Gretzky in 1984.

PART III
THE BIG YEARS

1907

The Tigers could not win a game in the World Series against the Chicago Cubs. The best they could get was one tie. This was the year Hughie Jennings established himself as a first-class manager. He was one of the first to use psychology on his players. He said: "You never waste your time and energy scolding a man in anger. When you are angry your reasoning is not sound. If you must scold a player, let him know that by taking up time with him you are paying him the highest compliment possible." This was the year Jennings disciplined Cobb for the only time in their careers. Cobb had gotten into a street fight and hurt his hand. He was able to play, but Jennings held him out for three days. When he allowed him back in the lineup, Cobb was burning so much to play that he hit a triple to win the game.

1908

Again the Tigers were beaten in the World Series—again by the Cubs. Cobb held out for $5,000. It was an unheard-of sum at the time. He got $4,500. The fans were drained from the long season and only 6,210 turned out for the final game. The owners, in a fit of generosity, gave each player an extra $145 from the receipts. This was the year they used four umpires for the first time in history. It was the year the Baseball Writers' Association of America was founded in Detroit. It was also the year Ty Cobb got his nickname: the Georgia Peach.

1909

The Tigers lost the World Series for the third straight year. This time the Pittsburgh Pirates beat them. Cobb won the home run title with nine.

Pitcher Babe Adams beat the Tigers three times in the Series. He got an unexpected chance to start the opener when Howard Camnitz, the Pittsburgh ace, was unable to pitch because of a bout with the bottle. Camnitz had been given $1,200 to stop drinking but failed to earn it. It was 32 degrees for one game in Detroit. Some of the players were looking for their own bottles. Adams was the hero and the women of the day were so taken by him that they followed him back to his hotel, camped on his doorstep, and wouldn't leave until he came out and gave them all a kiss.

1934

The Tigers wanted to get Babe Ruth from the Yankees to become their manager but couldn't work it out. At the suggestion of H. G. Salsinger, sports editor of *The Detroit News*, the Tigers got catcher Mickey Cochrane from Connie Mack of the Philadelphia A's and made him their manager.

Cochrane woke up the whole town, but the Tigers lost again in the World Series—this time to the St. Louis Cardinals. Commissioner Kenesaw Mountain Landis made history by pulling St. Louis leftfielder Joe Medwick off the field when the fans in the bleachers began pelting him with garbage after Medwick had slid in hard to Marv Owen at third base for the Tigers. It was a great day for Landis. He'd finally learned how to squirt tobacco juice through his teeth like Pepper Martin of the Cardinals and was showing off his newfound trick to everyone around him.

Up goes the 1934 pennant on Opening Day of 1935.

1935

The Yankees dumped Babe Ruth and he went to Boston, where his career came to an inglorious end. Cochrane, meanwhile, led the Tigers to their first World Championship, beating the Cubs in six games. The Tigers had to play without their big slugger, Hank Greenberg, who had broken his wrist. Owner Frank Navin ordered Cochrane to move Marv Owen from third to first and put the light-hitting Flea Clifton on third. The players objected and Goose Goslin went to Navin and issued a formal complaint. They felt Clifton was a sure out and, with Owen in a slump, it would be like having three pitchers in the lineup.

Navin's word stood. Clifton didn't get a hit in 16 tries and Owen got only one in 21 tries, but the others, including Cochrane, made up for it and beat the Cubs. Cochrane scored the winning run on a hit by Goslin.

Grantland Rice, the most celebrated sportswriter of his day, wrote of the Detroit victory: "The leaning tower can now crumble and find its level with the Pisan plain. The Hanging Gardens can grow up in weeds. Let time's ancient bough shed decaying worlds as the rattle of machine guns echo along Ethiopian trails. After 48 years, the Detroit Tigers at last are baseball champions of the world."

Mickey Cochrane comes across with the game-winning run on Goose Goslin's single to clinch the 1935 World Series.

Fans file out quietly after Tigers wrap up the World Series in 1935.

1940

Nobody expected the Tigers to win a pennant this year. The club was down. It was trying to recover from the shock of losing Mickey Cochrane, both as a player and a manager. Cochrane had been beaned by Yankee pitcher Bump Hadley and forced to leave the game. Charlie Gehringer was getting old and gone were such old-time heroes as Goose Goslin, Jo-Jo White, and Gee Walker. But they got some heavy hitting from Rudy York and Hank Greenberg and picked up Bobo Newsom in a trade. Newsom posted a 21–5 mark, and the Tigers finished on top, with a rookie named Floyd Giebell pitching the deciding game in Cleveland and beating Bob Feller on the final Friday of the season.

They lost the World Series again, with shortstop Dick Bartell holding a relay from the outfield in a critical spot of the final game against Cincinnati.

1945

This was the craziest season of all—the last of the wartime years. St. Louis had a one-armed player named Pete Gray. The Yankees had two outfielders named Johnny Lindell and Hershel Martin, who ran into each other one day, and Lindell spiked his teammate on the nose. Jimmie Foxx, the old slugger, pitched for the Philadelphia Phillies, and Nate Andrews came out of Alcoholics Anonymous and had a good year for the Boston Braves, falling off the wagon again the next year. It was into this bizarre situation that Hank Greenberg returned from the army and won the pennant for the Tigers by hitting a grandslam home run in the rain on the final day of the season in St. Louis. When the Tigers took their motley collection of players to Chicago to play the motley collection of Cubs, they asked Chicago columnist Warren Brown who would win. He replied: "I don't think either team can win." The Tigers prevailed in seven games and they still talk about Chuck Hostetler, who fell down rounding third base in a critical moment and was tagged out. He represented all that was zany in 1945.

1968

An incredible year for the Tigers. Nobody hit .300 and yet they ran away with the pennant. They won games in every possible manner. They won them on grand-slammers, bloop singles, and even triple plays. At times, especially when Denny McLain was pitching, they could do no wrong. Denny won 31 times and lost only 6. He became the game's first 30-game winner since Dizzy Dean in 1934. It was a wild party for all of them. The players frolicked everywhere they went and manager Mayo Smith let them go their way. After all, they were beating everyone in sight. Smith made a bold move when he put centerfielder Mickey Stanley at shortstop in the World Series so he could get Al Kaline back into his outfield. Kaline had missed much of the season due to injury. It was a dangerous gamble, but it worked, and the Tigers beat the Cardinals in the Series after being down three games to one.

A keeper: Sparky Anderson with dark hair.

1972

Billy Martin was the manager and he took the aging Tigers—the heroes of '68—and squeezed one more good season out of them. The Tigers won the Eastern Division but were beaten by Oakland in the playoffs. The players went on strike, walking out at the end of spring training and not coming back until the 14th day of the season. Martin fought with everyone around him. He taunted the umpires and slugged a fan. He argued with his players and the writ-

ers. But he turned out a winner. In the playoffs, Oakland shortstop Bert Campaneris got angry when Lerrin LaGrow dusted him off and he threw his bat at LaGrow, just missing him. Campaneris was suspended, but Oakland won anyway, taking the final game in Detroit by a 2–1 score. Martin was screaming to the end, claiming the umpires missed a call at first base, which allowed Oakland to score the winning run.

Second baseman Dick McAuliffe celebrates the '72 victory by—what else?—sitting in the Coke case.

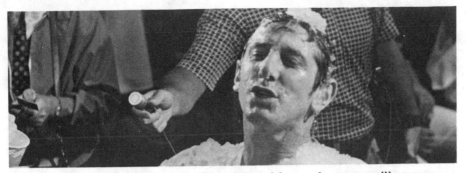

Billy Martin, the manager in '72, giving his postgame soliloquy.

1984

Another incredible season, this time because the Tigers started with a 35–5 record and absolutely destroyed the rest of the league. Jack Morris pitched a no-hitter in April and didn't talk to the press all through the summer. Morris won once in the playoffs and twice in the World Series and was the pitching leader that manager Sparky Anderson always thought he could be. The Tigers made a trade in spring training in which they sent Glenn Wilson and John Wockenfuss to the Philadelphia Phillies for relief pitcher Willie Hernandez and Dave Bergman. All Hernandez did was post a 9–3 record with 32 saves and win both the MVP and Cy Young awards.

The fans rioted on the night of the Tigers' World Series victory over San Diego and the next day Sparky Anderson promised the city his team would win again in 1985. The Tigers didn't, but Sparky kept on talking and promised his team would come back in 1986.

Hooray! Sparky says there'll be no more curfews.

FRED SMITH IS CONSIDERED THE FOREMOST HISTORIAN OF BASEBALL IN DETROIT. HE HAS FOLLOWED THE TIGERS SINCE 1925.

HERE ARE SOME OF HIS FAVORITE TRIVIA QUESTIONS AND ANSWERS:

Q. WHAT WAS LANCE PARRISH'S ORIGINAL POSITION WHEN HE BROKE INTO ORGANIZED BASEBALL?

A. PARRISH BROKE IN WITH BRISTOL IN 1974 AS A THIRD BASEMAN.

Q. WHERE AND HOW DID MARK "THE BIRD" FIDRYCH GET HIS NICKNAME?

A. IT WAS HUNG ON HIM AT BRISTOL IN 1974 BY COACH JEFF HOGAN. HOGAN DUBBED HIM THAT BECAUSE FIDRYCH REMINDED HIM OF BIG BIRD ON THE "SESAME STREET" TV SHOW.

Q. WHO TOOK OVER FOR AL KALINE IN RIGHT FIELD AFTER HE RETIRED?

A. LEON ROBERTS. THE YEAR WAS 1975.

Q. WHO IS THE ONLY TIGER EVER TO HIT A HOME RUN WITH THE BASES LOADED IN THE WORLD SERIES?

A. JIM NORTHRUP. HE DID IT IN THE SIXTH GAME OF THE 1968 SERIES AGAINST THE ST. LOUIS CARDINALS, CONNECTING OFF LARRY JASTER.

Q. WHO WAS THE OLDEST TIGER TO PLAY IN A GAME?

A. ROGER (DOC) CRAMER WAS 43 WHEN HE PLAYED THE OUTFIELD AND FIRST BASE FOR THE TIGERS IN 1948.

Q. WHAT NUMBER DID AL KALINE WEAR WHEN HE JOINED THE TIGERS IN 1953?

A. THEY GAVE HIM NO. 25 AND THEN PAT MULLIN'S NO. 6 WHEN MULLIN RETIRED IN 1954.

I'll get by with a little help from my friends.

ALL-TIME TIGER TEAM

1B—Hank Greenberg
2B—Charlie Gehringer
SS—Alan Trammell
3B—George Kell
OF—Ty Cobb
OF—Harry Heilmann

OF—Al Kaline
C—Mickey Cochrane
P—Hal Newhouser
RP—John Hiller
Manager—Mickey
  Cochrane

Few cities have had as many great players as Detroit. Or for a more extended length of time.

No decade has passed in the 20th century without the Tigers boasting at least one exceptional ball player—a standout for all time.

They had Ty Cobb early in the century, lighting up the first two decades in Detroit with his awesome abilities. He was followed by Harry Heilmann and Charlie Gehringer in the 1920s. Gehringer linked up with Mickey Cochrane and Hank Greenberg in the thirties, and Greenberg went on to star into the 1940s.

George Kell and Hal Newhouser made their mark in the 1940s and 1950s, and Al Kaline was a standout in three decades—the fifties, sixties, and seventies. Now, in the 1980s, we have been gifted with the talents of Alan Trammell.

These nine players, plus relief pitcher John Hiller from the 1970s, comprise the All-Time Tiger Team, as selected by a special panel of baseball observers in the summer of 1985.

It was time to bring the team up to date, to bring it into modern times. The job was done by Rick Ferrell, the longtime catcher, scout, coach, and front-office worker of the Tigers; Ernie Harwell, the Tigers' broadcaster; Lyall Smith, the former sports editor of the *Detroit Free Press*; Edgar Hayes, the former sports editor of *The Detroit Times*; Joe Falls, sports editor of *The Detroit News*, and Eli Zaret—the rookie—the young sportscaster from the Tigers' TV station, WDIV-TV.

Together they represented nearly 250 years of watching major-league baseball, and together they chose a team that should stand the test of time. A profile of each player follows.

- *Hank Greenberg, first base:* A prodigious slugger, he could hit them deep into the upper deck. His RBI figures were staggering by today's standards— 170, 183, 146, and 150. He challenged Babe Ruth's record with 58 homers in 1938. Greenberg would take batting practice, with kids shagging for him, until his hands bled from the effort. He was tall, gangling, and flat-footed, and the game did not come easy to him. He came out of the service in the 1945 season and hit his memorable homer in the rain at St. Louis to clinch the pennant on the final day of the season. He was the first great Jewish player in Detroit and was the target of unmerciful riding. He answered his critics with one more towering shot into the left-field seats. They finally called him "Hammerin' Hank."

- *Charlie Gehringer, second base:* From 1926 through 1942, this man compiled one of the most distinguished records of all time. Gehringer had a career average of .320 and was the backbone of three pennant winners. He batted .356 in 1934 and followed with .330, .354, and .371. He did it all without saying two words a day. He let his actions speak for him. He was born in Fowlerville, Michigan, and a big night on the town was playing Ping-Pong at the Detroit YMCA. He loved golf and played the game as he batted—left-handed. When his townsfolk gave him a set of right-handed golf clubs, he simply turned around and played the game right-handed. A nearly flawless fielder, he covered the right side of the infield in the same manner Lou Whitaker does for the modern-day Tigers.

- *Alan Trammell, shortstop:* He has been at it for only nine years but has moved ahead of all the other shortstops in Detroit history. Trammell has done it with consistent hitting, superb fielding, and a love of the game that makes him seem like the eternal kid down at the corner sandlot. He has won four Gold Glove awards. He batted .364 in the 1984 playoff against Kansas City and .450 in the World Series against San Diego. He was voted the Most Valuable Player in the Series. He also was voted the smartest player in a poll of American League managers. He has batted .300 three times and is a very popular player in the clubhouse. He used to sneak under the fence to watch the Padres play in San Diego. In the World Series he hit a ball over the fence against the Padres. He has been handicapped by injuries but plays through them.

- *George Kell, third base:* The young fans of today know this man as the one who calls the plays on TV for the Tigers. He used to make the plays at third base—off his chest, off his arms, off his legs. George Kell got in front of everything and threw batters out at first with great regularity. Even when Joe DiMaggio broke his jaw with a vicious shot down the third baseline, Kell was able to retrieve the ball and get Joe D. by a step before collapsing into a heap. Kell was the first third baseman in American League history to win a batting title. He did it in 1949, beating out Ted Williams on the final day of the season by two ten-thousandths of a point: .3429 to .3427. Kell batted .340 the next season and finished with a .306 mark for 15 seasons.

- *Ty Cobb, outfield:* Many consider this man the greatest player in history. His achievements were awesome. The modern-day player considers .280 a solid batting average. Cobb hit .300 in 23 major-league seasons. He won 12 American League batting championships in a 13-year period. At one time he held 90 major-league records. One of them is the highest career average in history: .367. He still holds that record. And yet, he was not a large man. He played with an intensity that could frighten those around him. He was an all-out competitor who devised every method he could think of to beat you— including flashing his spikes in your face and sometimes sinking them into your ankles.

- *Harry Heilmann, outfield:* They called him "Old Slug," and for 34 years— 17 in the batter's box and 17 in the broadcast booth—he thrilled fans with his great style. Only Ty Cobb ever out-hit him on the Tigers. Heilmann learned from the master and gave him credit for his lifetime mark of .342. He won four batting championships, oddly enough in odd-numbered years— 1921, 1923, 1925, and 1927. He had averages of .394, .403, .393, and .398. In the even-numbered years, he batted .356, .346, .367, and .328. He began his broadcasting career in 1934 and told the city of two straight pennants and the World Series championship in his inimitable fashion. He was short on statistics and long on stories. He liked to tell of the time he won the batting title on the final day, getting seven hits in nine at bats in a doubleheader.

- *Al Kaline, outfield:* For 22 years this man conducted himself with great presence in Detroit. The game wasn't as easy as it seemed for him. Kaline had to battle for everything. When he was a skinny kid, he didn't think he could hit, so he taught himself to field—until he became the finest outfielder in the history of the Tigers. He had a strong and accurate arm. At the plate, he battled the pitchers on every pitch and took his modest talents to a career average of .297, with 3,007 hits. He played with many injuries, including disfigured toes from a birth defect. He batted .379 in his only World Series. He also hit 399 home runs, which surprised a lot of people. He didn't have that much muscle. He simply worked at his hitting and outthought the pitchers on many occasions. He was the youngest American League batting champion ever, taking the title at 19 with a .340 average in 1955.

- *Mickey Cochrane, catcher/manager:* Here is the Spirit of Detroit. On the field, he pushed them to peak performance. In the dugout, he led them to one victory after another. Black Mike was a tough competitor, a ruddy-faced Irishman who could bat first because he ran so fast, whistle doubles into the right-field corner, score ahead of Gehringer and Greenberg, and then handle his pitchers with an iron will while throwing out every base runner in sight. He batted .320 for 13 years in the majors, with a .313 mark in his four playing seasons in Detroit. His career here was brief, but effective. His drive and desire touched people everywhere, including an Oklahoma miner who listened to the Tigers win the '35 World Series and was so impressed that he knew he had picked the right name for his son—Mickey Mantle.

- *Hal Newhouser, pitcher:* You may call him "Prince Hal," for that's what he was—a true stylist in his day. Bob Feller would come at you with that high kick and that blazing fastball, mixed in with his wicked curve. He was the farm boy toiling in the fields. Prince Hal was a man of royalty, a man of high manner and morals. He was leaner and meaner, a tremendous competitor, giving in to no man or team. They say his curve made noise as it crackled across the plate. Prince Hal won 200 games with the Tigers, including another 7 in his twilight years with Cleveland. That gave him a major-league mark of 207-150. He had a 29-9 record in 1944 and 25-9 in 1945. Some demeaned his marks because they came during the war years. When the servicemen returned in 1946, Prince Hal posted a 26-9 record. He is still in love with baseball and scouts the college and high school ranks.
- *John Hiller, relief pitcher:* This man's story is one of the most stirring in Detroit history. First, he saved himself, then he saved the Tigers. Hiller was not a very pleasant man when he joined the Tigers in 1965. He was selfish and self-centered. By his own admission, he thought of little more than himself. Then, in 1971, he was felled by a heart attack. It changed his life, his whole philosophy of living. He began thinking of others, and in the process he became the finest relief pitcher Detroit has ever known. Hiller pitched for the Tigers for 15 years. He wound up with 125 saves and a lifetime ERA of 2.83. When he left, he stood in front of the Detroit dugout and applauded the people in the stands. He was thanking "them" for putting up with "him." It was one of the most touching moments ever seen in the Detroit ballpark.

Here is the batting order Sparky Anderson would use for the All-Time Tiger Team:

1. *Charlie Gehringer:* "A great line-drive hitter—he'd be on base all day long."
2. *George Kell:* "He could shoot the ball into right field every time up. He could even do it while eating lunch."
3. *Ty Cobb:* "The best hitter on the club, so I've got to put him where I can get the most out of him."
4. *Hank Greenberg:* "My lumber man. With this lineup, he could get 400 RBI a year."
5. *Harry Heilmann:* "A great-great hitter. He'd give them all kinds of trouble, and he'd make them pitch to Greenberg."
6. *Mickey Cochrane:* "I'd like a left-handed hitter in this spot, and he was a great left-handed hitter. They talk about his catching, but he was outstanding with the bat."
7. *Al Kaline:* "I'd like a little speed in this spot, and Al could run with the best of them. He could spray the ball around and keep our rallies going."
8. *Alan Trammell:* "He has to hit eighth in this lineup, but he is so consistent in everything he does he would help us in every inning of every game."
9. *Hal Newhouser:* "I've been looking for a great left-handed pitcher, and here

he is. They tell me there were days they couldn't touch him."

Relief pitcher: "John Hiller was a workhorse and could go long or short for you. Imagine a John Hiller and then a Willie Hernandez in your bullpen. They'd make you look like a genius."

Comment: "Let me manage this team, and I'll ask Jim Campbell for a lifetime contract."

GIBSON'S GONERS

Kirk Gibson hit them everywhere except off the Ambassador Bridge. Here are some of his tape-measure homers of 1985:

- *April 10*—Off the facing of the third deck in Tiger Stadium, 80 feet from the ground
- *May 10*—Over the roof off Tom Seaver of the White Sox, his second out-of-the-park shot in Detroit
- *May 15*—A drive into the football press box in right field of the Minny Dome in Minneapolis
- *May 21*—Over the center-field fence in Anaheim
- *May 31*—Into the right-center-field bleachers, upstairs, in Tiger Stadium
- *June 4*—Off the right-field light tower in Tiger Stadium, nearly 100 feet high
- *June 16*—A towering drive off the back row of seats in the bleachers at Yankee Stadium, estimated at 500 feet
- *June 19*—Off the facing of the third deck in right field in Detroit
- *July 1*—An opposite field shot to left in Baltimore, the ball striking the seats in the second deck near the foul pole
- *August 3*—A massive shot off the roof in right field in Tiger Stadium, the ball bouncing back on the field
- *September 3*—Another third-deck shot in Detroit

Tigers with Game-Winning RBIs
(since this statistic was started in 1980)

Lance Parrish, 61	Chet Lemon, 28
Lou Whitaker, 49	Larry Herndon, 25
Kirk Gibson, 43	Steve Kemp, 20
Alan Trammell, 38	John Wockenfuss, 20
Tom Brookens, 31	Darrell Evans, 17

BASEBALL'S WINNINGEST MANAGERS
OF THE 20TH CENTURY

Sparky Anderson moved from 18th place to 13th place in the all-time standings in 1985, moving ahead of Earl Weaver, Wilbert Robinson, Jimmie Dykes, Miller Huggins, and Al Lopez. However, he lost 6 games to Gene Mauch, who won 90 with the California Angels, while Sparky won 84 with the Tigers. Mauch moved from 11th to 9th place.

- Connie Mack, 3,776
- John McGraw, 2,840
- Bucky Harris, 2,159
- Joe McCarthy, 2,126
- Walter Alston, 2,040
- Leo Durocher, 2,010
- Casey Stengel, 1,926
- Bill McKechnie, 1,898
- Gene Mauch, 1,641

- Ralph Houk, 1,619
- Fred Clarke, 1,602
- Clark Griffith, 1,491
- **Sparky Anderson, 1,426**
- Al Lopez, 1,422
- Miller Huggins, 1,413
- Jimmie Dykes, 1,407
- Wilbert Robinson, 1,397
- Earl Weaver, 1,395

What does Sparky think? Does he think he can catch John McGraw?

"I'd have to be a hundred years old to catch him . . . and I'd have to be 200 to catch Connie Mack," says the Detroit manager.

PHILADELPHIA PHILLIES
SECOND BASE

I like the bubble gum cards better since they took my playing record off them and put on my managing record.

—Sparky Anderson

1968: GO GET 'EM TIGERS

It seemed so easy in 1968. The Tigers had a solid team plus the best pitcher in baseball and they seemed to frolic through the entire season without much trouble. After all, didn't Denny McLain win 31 games? Didn't the Tigers finish 12 games ahead of the Baltimore Orioles?

It wasn't that easy.

First of all, there was great apprehension in the city in the spring of 1968. It was a year after the riot of 1967—a year when the city burned as no city ever has in the history of this country. Forty-three people died in the riot of 1967 and millions upon millions of dollars were lost in damaged property.

Everyone was scared in the spring of 1968—scared it might happen again.

They went out and bought guns and other weapons to defend themselves so that in the spring of 1968 Detroit was an armed camp. Not many people were thinking of the baseball team; they were concerned with their own safety.

Then, too, the frustration of 1967, when the Tigers lost the pennant on the final day—indeed, in the final inning of the final day, with Dick McAuliffe, the final batter, jamming into a rally-killing, inning-ending, season-ending double play—was still in the air, and the fans were not happy with the Tigers when they came back to play in 1968. They booed them until the middle of the season and were still on first baseman Norm Cash all the way into August. It wasn't easy at all in 1968.

The club suffered injuries at every

Mickey Lolich is a load for catcher Bill Freehan, but who cares? The look on Dick McAuliffe's face says it all—the Tigers are champions in 1968.

The '68 champs look like kids: Dick McAuliffe (left) and Denny McLain in the front and Norm Cash, Al Kaline, and Bill Freehan in the back.

turn. Al Kaline went out with a fractured arm. He missed almost three months. Pitcher Earl Wilson needed crutches to get around on a jammed foot. Willie Horton was knocked unconscious in a collision with shortstop Ray Oyler, who was 45 pounds lighter than Willie. Later, Horton hurt his foot and had to come out of the lineup. Don Wert, the third baseman, was beaned. Eddie Mathews, the old pro from the National League, suffered a herniated disc in his back and missed almost the entire season. Wilson was hit twice by line drives in the same inning. The first was a triple-carom shot off his shoulder, jaw, and thumb. McAuliffe, the scrappy second baseman, got into a fight with

The smallest crowd ever to see the Tigers was 404. It was for a game against Boston on September 24, 1928.

They sold only 18 hot dogs that day. Please don't look it up.

Chicago pitcher Tommy John, and the whole team brawled with the Oakland A's in a beanball contest. One of the players wound up hitting a woman in the stands with a ball and she filed a damage suit for $200,000 against the Tigers.

Yet, there was a spirit on this team that carried the Tigers through all of

Better days for Denny McLain and his family.

When the Yankees clinched the pennant in Detroit in 1928, Babe Ruth wanted to throw a party. He asked the hotel to send a piano up to his suite.

They said they didn't have one.

The Babe went out and bought one.

own wild kind of lifestyle, but he pulled them all along with him on the strength of his incredible pitching. He won thirty-one times and lost only six. In most of the games he was a mismatch for the opposition. The Tigers won so easily when he was out there that the whole season seemed easy.

No player in Detroit history ever had the kind of season McLain had in 1968, on and off the field—especially off.

On the second day of the season, he showed up with a mop of red hair. "What's the fuss?" he asked. "I've always had red hair."

He ripped the fans one night, calling them the worst in baseball after they had booed him. Later, he said

their troubles. It was almost as if it was their turn to win and they all knew it.

Denny McLain set the tone for the 1968 season.

He went his own way, creating his

he meant only a portion of the fans. It was too late. He had put his foot in his mouth and had embarrassed himself and the Detroit ball club.

Denny didn't care. He kept right on rolling.

- *June 13:* His blond hair came back. He said: "I did not dye my hair red, no matter what anyone says. It was Mother Nature."
- *July 7:* After winning the first game of a doubleheader, Denny climbed to the third deck and serenaded the fans on the organ during the second game. He gave them his rendition of "Satin Doll." He said: "What's the matter with the amplifier? I'll send a man out to check it."
- *July 10:* He pitched two scoreless innings at the All-Star game, after flying in from Las Vegas in a borrowed Lear jet. He flew back after the game, leaving teammate Mickey Lolich without a ride after promising him one.
- *July 31:* He won his 21st game with a shutout and, when asked about pitching in Tiger Stadium, said: "I hate it. I hate it. I hate it." A new organ was delivered to his home that afternoon.
- *August 14:* He won number 24 and said *Time* and *Life* were after him and Ed Sullivan and Joey Bishop wanted him on their TV shows.
- *September 1:* He beat Baltimore in a big game and started a triple play. He said that if he didn't snag Boog Powell's liner, it would have smashed into his face and broken his eyeglasses. He said he was lucky to be alive. The next day, newspaper pictures showed him catching the ball at belt level.
- *September 9:* Denny spent the day with the Smothers Brothers.
- *September 14:* He won number 30 and came back on the field and doffed his cap to the jubilant fans, who were crying out: "Denny! Denny! Denny!" Denny was asked how he planned to celebrate. "My wife and I will figure out something," he winked.

Even then they wasted champagne as Norm Cash—he's the one with the tongue—gags it up with John Hiller after the pennant is won in 1968.

1984: BLESS YOU BOYS

Jim Hawkins used to be a baseball writer for the *Detroit Free Press*. He quit his job and became rich.

At least he did in the summer of 1984.

He opened a novelty shop called The Fan-Attic and sold everything he could put a Tiger logo on: caps, jackets, pennants, pens, pencils, pins, bats, balls, gloves, glasses, rugs, wastebaskets, and even potty seats.

Nobody ever saw a baseball season in Detroit like 1984.

"I still can't believe what happened," says VP Jim Campbell. "I mean, if you were to tell me you'd ever have a season where you won 35 of your first 40 games and nobody

Marty Castillo gets a big greeting from Chet Lemon after hitting his homer in the '84 World Series. The National League ump doesn't seem too happy about it.

Most World Series Games Won by Managers

Casey Stengel, 37
Joe McCarthy, 30
John McGraw, 26
Connie Mack, 24
Walter Alston, 20
Miller Huggins, 18
Sparky Anderson, 16

Among our souvenirs. . . .

would get hurt and the weather would be perfect and you'd draw 2.7 million fans and win the division, the pennant, and the World Series, I'd say you were crazy."

That was 1984: a crazy season.

Never did the City of Detroit take to the Tigers as it did in 1984. Everybody became a Tiger fan. The bandwagon started rolling early and everybody jumped on. DJs did nothing but talk about the Tigers. The same with the 11 o'clock anchors. Moms, dads, kids, aunts, grandfathers, grandmothers, uncles, cousins, friends, relatives—they all fell in love with the Tigers.

Why not?

The team was very exciting. Jack Morris pitched a no-hitter on national TV on the first Saturday of the season and the whole country started paying attention to what was going on in Detroit.

What was going on was a baseball team playing the kind of ball that simply took people's breath away.

The Tigers won 35 of their first 40 games for the fastest start in history and they stayed in first place from wire to wire.

Don Demeter had a streak of 266 games without an error. It came to an end when a dog ran onto the field and distracted him into making a wild throw.

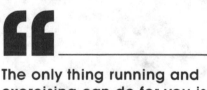

The only thing running and exercising can do for you is make you healthy.
—Mickey Lolich

The marketplace became flooded with Tiger bread, Tiger cheese, Tiger books, Tiger Christmas ornaments, Tiger shirts, Tiger socks—Tiger mania that would have dazzled the likes of Ty Cobb, Mickey Cochrane, and Denny McLain.

They never saw anything like the summer of 1984.

Neil Heffernann, owner of a souvenir store near the ballpark, said: "My hands got sore from picking buttons off the board."

A new drink was invented—Tiger Fever—a wine cooler that added to the fun of the summer.

Tiger Home-Run Champions

1908: Sam Crawford, 7
1909: Ty Cobb, 9
1914: Sam Crawford, 8
   (tied for league lead)
1935: Hank Greenberg, 36
   (tied for league lead)
1938: Hank Greenberg, 58
1940: Hank Greenberg, 41
1943: Rudy York, 34
1946: Hank Greenberg, 46
1985: Darrell Evans, 40

The picture that made Detroit infamous: burning of the police car after the '84 World Series ended.

The club had a new owner, Pizza King Tom Monaghan, but he wisely stayed out of the way and let it all happen. He simply became their biggest fan. He arrived in a helicopter just before game time and left the same way. He flew in over the heads of the people out on the street waiting to buy tickets.

He was very visible. "Why not?" he said. "Maybe I can sell a few more pizzas along the way." He opened so many new shops that his profits rose to incredible heights.

The Tigers got Willie Hernandez from the Phillies in spring training, and he became the most dominant player in the American League. He had a season to end all seasons. He was almost perfect out of the bullpen, compiling a 9–3 record with 32 saves. He won the MVP award as well as the Cy Young award and some nights the batters couldn't get the ball past the pitcher's rubber against him.

The Tigers didn't have a 20-game winner, but it didn't matter. Jack Morris won 19, Dan Petry 18, and Milt Wilcox 17. The Tigers hit 187 home runs and led the league in scoring. They won the division by 15 games, beat Kansas City three straight in the playoffs and San

Roger Craig (left) celebrates the 1984 pennant clinching with Aurelio Lopez and Don Petry. Don't get too high, guys.

You should see her shirt for "John B. Whitaker."

Diego in five games in the World Series. They met every test, handled every challenge. The cry of "Bless you, boys" rang throughout the entire city.

And then it was 1985 and the Tigers fell to third place. A lot of people stopped coming to the ballpark. Jim Hawkins closed up his novelty shop and turned his attention to a business he could always count on in good times and bad.

He opened a bar.

For Numbers Nuts Only

The Tigers were at their best in 1985 on Tuesdays. They had a 14-7 record on Tuesday. The team's worst day was Monday, when they were 7-14.

Please don't ask what this all means.

The victory parade moves along Congress as Detroit says
"thank you" to the 1984 champions.

1984: A QUOTABLE YEAR

- *April 7*—Sparky Anderson, after they made the Tigers stand around in the cold for 20 minutes during the opening-game ceremonies in Comiskey Park, Chicago: "They forgot two things. Let's introduce the wives and grandparents. Everybody else has been introduced."
- *April 20*—Dan Quisenberry, relief pitcher of the Kansas City Royals: "I picked the Tigers to win last year and I wound up picking my nose. But I pick them again this season."
- *April 21*—Frank White, Kansas City second baseman, after the Tigers' first loss: "I'm sure the streak was fun for them while it lasted, but I don't think anyone has won 162 in a row. You could look it up."
- *May 8*—Alan Trammell, shortstop, with the Tigers 24-4 in the standings: "I've run out of things to say because we're always winning. I'm saying the same things every time."
- *May 9*—Dan Quisenberry, after a grandslam by Trammell: "That's a longer ground ball than I usually give up."
- *May 24*—A fan from Dayton, talking to Sparky Anderson: "Sparky Anderson! I'm from Dayton. When you managed in Cincinnati, I was a big fan of yours. By the way, what are you doing now?"
- *June 7*—Sparky Anderson: "Nothing upsets me more than someone saying the pressure is beginning to build. I always thought pressure was having four kids and you're out of work and there's no money in the bank."

Everybody loves a parade—except the garbagemen.

A manager's dream: "Here comes Brown scoring, here comes Smith, here comes Jones, here comes. . . ."

- *June 19*—Billy Consolo, after his fan club, the Consolo Mios, doubled in size: "I got a letter from Southfield and one from Windsor. Business is booming."
- *July 3*—Alan Trammell, about the sore arm that sidelined him for more than a month: "I don't think it's serious."
- *July 19*—Sparky: "If I worried about every player who got upset, I'd be a raving maniac by now."
- *July 25*—Tom Brookens, when Doug Baker borrowed his bat and got four hits: "I'm glad to see my bat get some hits. There should be some in there."
- *July 30*—Gates Brown: "This team is more reserved than our 1968 team. It's a lot quieter. Our record speaks for itself. Ray Oyler dropped dead, Norm Cash had a stroke, and couple of other guys had heart attacks. I'm telling you, there was a lot of hard living."
- *August 31*—Lance Parrish: "It's not my job to go out there and reprimand Jack Morris every time he acts up like he shouldn't. He's a big boy."
- *September 3*—Lance Parrish, after a bad road trip: "I was 1 for the West Coast."
- *September 10*—Sparky: "Every time Bobby Cox calls his bullpen, he gets the wrong number."
- *October 8*—Dan Petry: "I don't care if we have to go to China to play. We're in the World Series."

This is one way to sweep a series.

PART IV
INSIDE THE CLUBHOUSE

===== **BASEBALL TALK** =====

Poor Tom Monaghan. The new owner of the Tigers didn't know what to do. His team had won it all for him in 1984, but in the middle of the 1985 season, the Tigers were struggling to stay even.

Monaghan called John Fetzer at his home in Kalamazoo. He had bought the club from Fetzer for $53 million in 1983.

"John, what'll I do?" he said. "We're losing."

"Do what I do," said Fetzer.

"What's that?" asked Monaghan.

"Just sit down, put your feet up, and bleed."

Sparky Goes 0-for-5

Sparky Anderson has five World Series rings—three of them winners. But he doesn't wear any of them in honor of Lefty Phillips, the old Los Angeles Dodgers scout and coach who died about 10 years ago. "They really belong to him, so how can I wear them?" says Sparky. "He taught me everything I know about baseball—baseball and life. The rings are his. I wouldn't dare wear them in public."

INSIDE LANCE PARRISH

Pet peeve: People who call him "Larry Parrish."

Favorite food: "Three-way tie: spaghetti, ravioli, and lasagna."

First big job: Bodyguard for Tina Turner at age of 20. "All I had to do was follow her around and make sure no one bothered her. It was more fun than work."

Favorite city: Anaheim. "I used to live there and I know people."

Least favorite city: Cleveland. "It's a dead town."

Learned his work habits from: His father, Otto, who was a deputy sheriff for Los Angeles County.

Superstition: He insists on wearing No. 13. He has been wearing it since the age of 13 in Little League. "I think I hit better on Friday the 13th. One Friday the 13th in high school, I intercepted three passes and kicked a school-record punt." He is so superstitious that it is written in his contract that he gets to wear No. 13.

"Oh, my, why did he throw that one?"

Hobbies: Golf, sketching, and drawing.
Toughest pitcher to face: Charlie Hough.
Favorite athlete: Ted Williams.
Turnoffs: Rude, ignorant people.
Favorite TV show: "The Young and the Restless."
Married: Arlyne Nolan after the 1978 season while playing winter ball in Puerto Rico. She was a former Miss Diamond Bar, Miss Hollywood, Miss Southern California, and first runner-up in the Miss California contest. They had their wedding banquet at a Dairy Queen in the Virgin Islands, where they ate hamburgers.

Lance and Arlyne at home with daughter Ashley.

Political affiliation: None.

Favorite subject in school: History.

Favorite book: I, Judas.

Person he admires the most: His wife, who could have had a movie career but turned it down because "They asked her, at the age of 13, to appear in two bed scenes in a film involving Jay ["Dennis the Menace"] North. They told her Elizabeth Taylor did the same thing at 16, but she told them she wasn't Elizabeth Taylor."

Greatest achievement: Making it to the major leagues.

Before baseball career: Parrish signed a letter of intent to play football at UCLA.

Chose baseball instead because: "They offered me $60,000, and that got my attention in a hurry." Until signing with the Tigers, his only brush with them was when he was working out with the California Angels in Anaheim and saw Mickey Lolich's dirty uniform in a laundry bin.

Favorite charity: Cystic fibrosis.

"Okay, I'm taking all you people to dinner tonight."

BEST CLUBHOUSES

Milt Wilcox's six favorite clubhouses to get out to early in the afternoon when things are getting boring around the hotel:

1. *Texas*—"Great place to get out of the heat and you can drink a lot of Cokes before Sparky shows up."
2. *Anaheim*—"Very sturdy card tables."
3. *Seattle*—"Best candy in the league. You can't beat their malted milk balls."
4. *Minnesota*—"Outstanding deviled eggs. The clubhouse guy also has baseball guides from 1955, so you can have something to read when you sit down."
5. *Cleveland*—"The clubhouse is nicer than downtown Cleveland. You can even get illegal sandwiches when Sparky isn't looking."
6. *Oakland*—"Superb sunflower seeds. Sparky even chews those himself."

Afterthought: "Geez, I forgot Baltimore. Baltimore may be first. They've got a pinball machine in there."

Sonny Eliot, the amateur umpire, bellows: "Whatta ya mean, weathermen are all wet!?"

INSIDE KIRK GIBSON

Baseball heroes: None.
Superstitions: None.
Most difficult thing to do in baseball: "Avoid overswinging."

Kirk Gibson loves a parade.

On choosing baseball over football: "I never thought I made the wrong decision, not for one day, not for one minute, even in the bad times."

Training clothing: When he wants to sweat, he wears three cotton undershirts and a rubber jacket.

Father's occupation: Math teacher.

Pet peeve: Doesn't like being called a "star." "I want to be one of the best ball players, but I don't want to be called a 'star' or a 'superstar.'"

Yippee! Let's do it again.

Milestone: As a two-sport star, he was able to play his final year of football at Michigan State after signing a professional baseball contract with the Tigers.

Changes in personality: "When I first came into this game, I was a crazy man. 'Madman,' they called me. But I've calmed down. At times I'm even rational. I'm not a dirty player, but if you get in my way. I'll knock you down."

Hobbies: Hunting, fishing, riding his horses, and driving his boat.

Motivation: "I don't play for publicity. The people who love me don't care if I go 0 for 100."

Kirk Gibson's Michigan State Football Statistics

Catches—112
Yards—2,347
Touchdowns—24

He also played one season for the Spartans' baseball team and batted .390 with 16 homers and 52 RBIs in 48 games.

Prince Valiant when he played football at Michigan State.

Kirk Gibson is back home and everybody loves him, especially the ladies.

ON THE ROAD

What is it like traveling with the Tigers? It is big airplanes, fine hotels, and excellent restaurants. It is also 75 mph bus rides in from the airport, with everybody hanging on for dear life. It is flying into Toronto at three o'clock in the morning, only to find the airport closed by curfew. The plane has to detour to Hamilton, Ontario, with the team busing into Toronto. Lights out at 5:00 A.M.

The surprises are endless when you knock around with a ball club. It gets like a Fellini movie. Pack. Unpack. Pack. Unpack. Come on along. It's a lot of fun.

Kansas City is lovely. In Kansas City the room maids fold the toilet tissue so the ends come to a point and it's easy to pull out when you need it. They do this while you are away at the ballpark.

In Kansas City, though, they no longer leave little mints on your pillow at night. The rigors of the road can pile up very quickly.

Kansas City has a special place in your heart. When the airport was still on the edge of downtown, the pilot would taxi out to the end of the runway and sit there with the brakes locked while building up power in his engine. The plane would be vibrating like a coffeepot on a stove. Then—suddenly—the pilot would release the brakes and away you'd go. He had to get off to this flying start to make it over the buildings in downtown Kansas City.

It was in Kansas City in 1961 that the Tigers took off in a hailstorm and the plane—a four-engine jet—rolled over on its side and tossed people around the cabin. Pitcher Hank Aguirre broke into such a sweat that his shirt, tie, pants, and even his socks were drenched.

This trip the Tigers are on starts at Metro Airport, on something called Midway Airlines.

"What's Midway Airlines?" one of the players asks. "I never heard of Midway Airlines."

Another replies, "It's a little line from an island in the Pacific Ocean. They've got these planes left over from the war."

Ernie Harwell says: "I see our next flight is on Nordair."

Ernie shakes his head.

"I thought Nordair was a refrigerator company."

Not all of them like to fly. Willie Horton was terrified of airplanes. His teammates hardly helped him by locking him in the men's room on one trip. George Myatt, a coach in the Bob Scheffing days, absolutely refused to get on any airplane unless he had a minimum of six martinis. The Tigers' four-engine plane once lost an engine on the way to Kansas City and the pilot had to divert to Chicago. Third baseman Ray Boone wrote down the numbers on the wing of the plane, and when the team was leaving Kansas City three days later, he checked the numbers and found this was the plane that had lost an engine. He said to his teammates, "See you later." He took the train back to Detroit.

The Tigers made their first flight

in 1956. Air travel was still new to the major leagues and the players wanted to fly from Lakeland, Florida, to Houston, Texas, rather than take a train.

Owner Spike Briggs was against air travel, but he finally relented when he got the pilot to agree not to fly out over the Gulf of Mexico. The pilot had to follow the Florida coastline around to Texas, or it was no deal.

What did any of us know about air travel in those days? The Tigers

Jeffrey Brown, son of Ike, striking for better working conditions in 1972.

"We'd better get Willie up in the bullpen."

flew out of Lakeland in a twin-engine DC-3 and they loaded it up with everything they could carry—bags, equipment, and a full complement of players and press. They took off from little Drain Field in Lakeland, and the plane was so weighted down that it ran off the runway on takeoff. They were bumping along in a field, trying to get airborne when trainer Jack Homel looked across the aisle and saw the petrified look on the face of one of the newspapermen.

Homel started laughing.

"Your biggest story," he roared, "and you'll never be able to write it."

The plane lifted slowly into the skies.

Now, a lifetime later, the Tigers are on their way to Kansas City and the pilot turns off the "No Smoking" sign. Sparky Anderson immediately lights up his pipe.

The players pair off in groups. Some play cards, some play Tonk, a game of dice with action that never ceases. Some put on their earphones and jiggle in their seats all the way to Kansas City. A few go to sleep. Pitcher Jack Morris begins reading a copy of *Beef Cattle Science*.

A writer asks him: "What are you reading that for?"

Morris says: "Someday I hope to become a beef cattle scientist."

They all fight their fears in different ways. When George Cantor was covering the team for the *Detroit Free Press*, he always tried to sit where he could see Al Kaline.

"I figure nothing could ever happen to a plane that Al Kaline is on," Cantor explained.

Cantor also is the man who, during a tornado in Kansas City, asked George Kell if he could sit next to him in the TV booth.

"Sure," said Kell, "but why do you want to sit in here?"

Cantor explained: "I never heard of anyone getting killed by a tornado while telecasting a baseball game."

It is expensive on the road. Shrimp cocktails in Kansas City are $8.80. That's better than the drinks at the bar of the Hyatt Hotel in New York City. They're $9.90.

The menu at the Hyatt says: "One egg $5.50. Two eggs $6.50."

You say to the waitress: "Can you scramble that second egg for me?"

She doesn't laugh. She doesn't even smile.

Most of the players room by themselves. Only the rookies are willing to double up. They would have to pay for privacy and they can't afford it.

Alan Trammell says: "I didn't ask for it, but they put a single room in my contract, and I took it."

It is very quiet around the hotel in the morning and into the early afternoon. Guess who is sleeping? The players begin straggling into the coffee shop in the middle of the afternoon. That's when they have their only real meal of the day.

At the ballpark there is always a sumptuous feast awaiting them after the games, but it is gobbled down so quickly that it hardly seems as if they're eating at all. They are served such delicacies as lasagna, ribs, chicken, and roast beef—the idea being the finer the food, the bigger the tip for the clubhouse man.

MOST CHALLENGING LOBBIES

The four hotel lobbies former trainer Bill Behm found most challenging to sit around in:

1. *Minnesota*—"Good seats, very comfortable, but nobody is walking around, and there's nothing to see. We're the only ones staying at the hotel, so we end up looking at each other."
2. *Texas*—"Only two chairs, so you can't be the third guy to show up in the lobby. Serious lobby sitters have to get up early."
3. *Seattle*—"A tough lobby. It's up on the fourth floor and you don't get too many weirdos walking around on the fourth floor."
4. *Chicago*—"Too big. Too many places to sit. They've got so many entrances you can't cover them all."

INSIDE CHET LEMON

Worst luck: The first day he showed up in training camp with the Tigers, his car got hit by another car (he wasn't hurt).

Pet peeve: Going out to dinner with his family and being bothered by autograph seekers. "I don't mind signing autographs in the right circumstances. People in the neighborhood don't ask for them. They're intimidated by me. My wife gets more requests for my autograph than I do."

Favorite food: Chicken or pasta. Absolutely won't eat New England clam chowder.

On unwinding: "I have to have my music. It relaxes me. I like all kinds of music but especially soft music. Barbra Streisand is one of my favorites. I like movies, too. We have a VCR and collect old movies. I like things like *Rocky*, *The Champ*, and *Marathon Man*."

Chet Lemon relaxes at home.

Religion: Jehovah's Witness. He and Lou Whitaker leave the field before they play the National Anthem because their religion teaches them to be beholden to no one but the True God.

Childhood: "I played all day, every day, and never got tired of it. On a Saturday, I'd play for four teams . . . even the police station team . . . and loved every minute of it. We'd even play on concrete and I'd slide on the concrete and my mom would give it to me for tearing up my clothes."

On the Cleveland scoreboard: "I hate that scoreboard. Every time up, it shows your batting average. Every time you don't get a hit, the number drops. If I don't get a hit in four tries, I walk up to the plate with my eyes closed."

A hot one on the inside gets Chet Lemon.

Favorite TV shows: "The Price Is Right" and "Leave It to Beaver."

Goals: "I want to be judged by what I do every day. I believe in consistency. Most of all, I want to be remembered by my peers."

On batting lineup: "I don't want to lead off. You just come up too many times. In a long game, you can go 0 for 6, and afterward you think, 'Oh, my, I must be bad.' I'll hit anywhere else."

On unwinding: Sitting in the sauna and Jacuzzi in his home, then watching a movie on his big-screen TV.

"All those who think this is a great book about the Tigers, please raise your bats."

BEST SWIMMING POOLS

Sparky Anderson's six favorite swimming pools to sit around when he has time to sit around swimming pools:

1. *San Diego*—"The best pool and the best scenery and I don't mean the mountains."
2. *Houston*—"A great place to sweat. Bring a pail of ice because it will melt in 10 minutes and you can start drinking the water."
3. *St. Louis*—"Excellent. They sell hot dogs at poolside."
4. *Pittsburgh*—"Outstanding. The pool is on the roof of the hotel, 26 floors up, and you can catch the rays before they get down to the poor people below."
5. *Kansas City*—"Very restful, but you don't dare go to sleep because you might start snoring, and if you start snoring, your mouth opens and the players start dingle-dangling things into your mouth."
6. *Philadelphia*—"A superb setting. They've got three pop machines at poolside and one of them sells Mr. Pibb. The record is three Mr. Pibbs in one day."

Comment: "Naw, I never go into the water."

HOW TO HANDLE PUBLICITY

Sparky Anderson's five rules for handling the pressure of publicity while on the road:

1. Order room service whenever possible. Don't eat in any of the public dining rooms at the hotel.
2. Don't answer the phone. Live by the message light on your phone. Call down for messages and don't answer any of them unless they seem urgent.
3. Don't lounge around the lobby. Stay in your room as much as possible. Watch TV, play cards, study algebra.
4. Don't be rude to people, but keep walking if they besiege you for autographs.
5. Don't miss the team bus.

TRAVELING SECRETARY OF THE YEAR

Frank Contway is not a name that will be remembered in the history of the Tigers.

It's a name Jack Homel, the old trainer, will never forget.

Contway served as the traveling secretary of the Tigers in the middle 1950s. He was a good friend of Spike Briggs, the owner. They both liked to have a good time.

The Tigers were in New York City for a weekend series against the Yankees and it was late at night—maybe 2:00 A.M.—and Homel was asleep in his room at the Commodore Hotel.

The phone rang.

It was Frank Contway.

He was in high spirits from a night on the town and told Homel to come on down for a nightcap. No way, Homel told him. Didn't he know what time it was? Homel was going back to sleep.

In a few moments there was a knock on Homel's door. He got out of bed, mumbling to himself: "Now what?" He was naked.

The knocking continued. "Who is it?" he called out.

"It's me," said Contway. "Come on out . . . I wanna talk to you."

Homel opened the door a crack. Contway reached in and grabbed him by the wrist and pulled him into the hallway.

Click!

The door snapped shut behind Homel. It was locked. Contway let go of Homel's wrist. He saw the magic of the moment—this burly man standing there without a stitch of clothes on— and started roaring and walking away.

Homel panicked.

"Hey, where are you going? You can't leave me here!"

Bing!

The elevator light went on down the hall. Homel took off. He raced down the corridor, around the

BEST CITIES TO SLEEP IN

Gates Brown's five favorite sleeping cities:

1. *Anaheim*—"They've got all-night TV, so when you can't sleep you can get up and watch a movie and that puts you back to sleep."
2. *Kansas City*—"The radio plays soft music, and you can fall asleep and leave the radio on because you can't hear it."
3. *Toronto*—"The best double beds in the league."
4. *Cleveland*—"I like Cleveland a lot because when we're in Cleveland I can go back to Detroit and sleep."
5. *Arlington, Texas*—"The best air-conditioning in the league."

corner, and found a small linen closet. He slipped in. He could hear the people getting off the elevator. He looked around the closet. All that was in there was a sink and a damp washcloth draped over the edge of the sink.

He took the washcloth and placed it in front of him and there he stayed for the next hour.

Two people came by.

Each time he peeked out the door and whispered: "Psssst! Psssst!"

He had to get their attention before he could get anything else from them. They turned around and all they saw through the crack in the door was a large naked man standing there holding a washcloth in front of him.

Both took off and ran to their rooms.

Finally, somewhere around 3:00 A.M. Homel got a passer-by to stop long enough to hear Homel blurt out his story, and the guy went downstairs to get another key to Homel's room. He also brought him a bathrobe.

That was the year Jack Homel did not vote Frank Contway "traveling secretary of the year."

He did talk to him, though.

Nobody knows what he said.

BEST COFFEE SHOPS

Alan Trammell's four favorite coffee shops:

1. *Texas*—"Great milk shakes, great cheesecake."
2. *Boston*—"Best clam chowder. I hate clams that taste like pencil erasers."
3. *New York*—"Lousy coffee shop, but a great deli down the street where you can get pie à la mode with ice cream."
4. *Barb Trammell's Kitchen*—"Where you can get eggs and bacon, waffles, French toast, and a good-morning kiss."

It was tough for Hughie Jennings, the old Tiger manager, to face his players the night after he dove into a dimly lit swimming pool and found that it had been drained.

They kept looking at the bump on his head.

Here is advice from Dan Petry about making ice cream:

"My favorites are peach and chocolate, and I'm pretty good at it. The important thing is not to get electrocuted when you put the plug in."

INSIDE JACK MORRIS

Boyhood hero: Bob Gibson.

Ambition: "It's not to be on the cover of *Sports Illustrated.* To have a little inner peace will be just fine."

Jack Morris: pitcher at work.

Nickname: "The Count." (Just don't call him "Mount Morris." People do that when they talk about the way he blows up on the pitcher's mound and he can't stand the name.)

Favorite city: Seattle. "It's clean and there are a lot of things to do."

Least favorite city: Cleveland. "It's ugly."

Childhood: His dad taught him how to play ball almost before

"I'm going to get those ants."

he knew how to walk. If young Jack won a game, he'd get steak for dinner. If he didn't, it was hamburger.

Religion: Mormon. He attended Brigham Young.

Habits: "I don't smoke, but I can't say I don't take an occasional drink. I can be a weak person at times."

Married: To Carolyn, the girl who lived two blocks from his home in St. Paul. "We were best friends long before we were lovers."

Most memorable game: His no-hitter in 1984, in which he struck out Ron Kittle of the White Sox for the final out. After the no-hitter, he cracked: "I hope they don't expect me to do this all the time."

Lucky number: Four.

Political affiliation: Democrat.

Biggest turn-on: Ski jumping.

Biggest turnoff: Traffic. "I hate it when I'm in the car and it's five o'clock."

Person he admires most: His high school coach, Ron Causton.

Favorite way to spend a summer day: Cutting the lawn.

Favorite way to spend a winter day: Driving his snowmobile through the woods.

Hobby: Hunting.

Wife Carolyn says: "Jack is a very simple person. He may pitch a no-hitter, but he still takes out the garbage."

BEST BARBERSHOPS

Billy Consolo's three favorite barbershops when they had barbershops in the old days:

1. *Los Angeles*—"The shop where my dad worked—10 chairs, eight manicurists, four shine boys, and a thousand magazines. I never had to pay there."
2. *Chicago, Palmer House*—"Twenty-eight chairs, two barbers to a chair. The only place you could get a platoon haircut."
3. *Boston*—"Over on Jersey Street. They had only two chairs, but they never used clippers."

BEST PRESS BOXES

Tom Gage of *The Detroit News* spends more time in press boxes than anyone in town, so—naturally—he rates the press boxes for us:

1. *Detroit*—"We're up in the clouds, but it's home, and how can you beat the chocolate almond ice cream?"
2. *Cleveland*—"Lots of spiders, but best view in the league."
3. *Anaheim*—"Very comfortable and the view used to be great until they closed in the stadium."
4. *Kansas City*—"Best working conditions, but it's enclosed and you feel like you're in a fish bowl."
5. *Boston*—"The front row is fantastic. You can reach out and touch the left-field wall."
6. *Chicago*—"The fans make it fun."
7. *Baltimore*—"Model of efficiency."
8. *Milwaukee*—"Long live the bratwursts."
9. *Minnesota*—"Where they measure home runs to the foot."
10. *Toronto*—"Cooped up again with no air-conditioning. When the sun is out, you fry."

ASK A SILLY QUESTION . . .

The 10 most memorable questions ever put to Sparky Anderson:

1. "Did you have white hair at birth?"
2. "Do you plan to pose for *Penthouse*?"
3. "Who is going to win the Stanley Cup?"
4. "Would you buy a used car from yourself?"
5. "Did you ever hit one over the Berlin Wall?"
6. "Do you believe in belly buttons?"
7. "Are you voting for Reagan or Gromyko?"
8. "What's your favorite color?"
9. "Are you allergic to ivy?"
10. "Do you fill your pipe with Early American Rosin Bag?"

LAKELAND: SPRING PLAYGROUND

Ah, Lakeland, Florida—spring training home of the Tigers. What a marvelous place.

Where else but in Lakeland, the "Citrus Capital of the World," is it impossible to get a glass of fresh orange juice?

Where else but in Lakeland would Bill Faul, the ex-Tiger pitcher, pull his car up on the curb and turn on the signal lights and try to hypnotize his girlfriend as she sat in the doorway of his motel room.

Where else but in Lakeland would Frank Lary dump a pail of dead fish in the swimming pool of the Holiday Inn—and Billy Hoeft go wading for them at midnight?

The Tigers have trained in Lakeland since 1934, with three years out in Evansville, Indiana, (1943–45) because of wartime restrictions on travel.

It used to be a sleepy town, Lakeland. At one time the only things open after 7 P.M. were the phone booths. They had one movie house in town, and one spring all it showed was *The Ten Commandments*. Dave Diles, a Detroit telecaster, beat the rap. "I saw it one commandment at a time," he said.

Frank Lary did his best to keep things exciting in Lakeland.

One day he put a dead snake in the Yankee dugout, and everyone loved it when Casey Stengel took one look at the inert critter and came flying up the dugout steps.

Another night there was nothing to do and Lary persuaded some of his teammates to borrow the Greyhound bus standing in front of the Elks' Club and take it for a ride in the country.

This is the same Frank Lary who was low on gas one night and drove back to Lakeland at 90 mph so he could make it before his tank ran dry.

Isn't spring training exciting?

Lakeland is the place where Mark Fidrych, under the light of spring-time moon, made love to a local lass on the pitcher's mound in Marchant Stadium.

Lakeland is the place where Hank Aguirre hit his golf ball into a swamp and tried to play it out of the mouth of an alligator.

Lakeland is the place where the players used to put spiders, beetles, and ants into the shoes, socks, and pockets of Johnny Groth because Groth hated all kinds of bugs.

It's an interesting place, Lakeland. You ought to see it one of these years. They even play baseball down there.

Who says Kirk Gibson never strikes out?

INSIDE WILLIE HERNANDEZ

Loves: Fishing, jazz, and just sitting around at home with his family.

Idol: Roberto Clemente.

First pitching experience: When he was 18 years old.

Family: He was the seventh of nine children, growing up in the small Puerto Rican town of Aguada.

Childhood: His family was poor, his father working in a sugar cane factory, his mother as a hotel maid. He hated Christmas because he'd see his friends riding around on bicycles while all his parents could give him was a quarter. At the age of 15, he moved to Chelsea, Massachusetts, where he worked with his brother, Jimmy, loading a pickup truck with auto parts and tires and driving it to Portland, Maine. He earned $145 per week.

Salary: $550,000 in 1985, $850,000 in 1986, $950,000 in 1987, $1.1 million in 1988, and 1.2 million in 1989. He also gets a bonus of $50,000 every time the Tigers draw 2.4 million at the gate.

Contract stipulations: He cannot take part in fencing, skydiving, hang gliding, surfing, scuba diving, or ice hockey.

Willie Hernandez and the good life in Puerto Rico.

Milt Wilcox gets his revenge for all the days he was sent to the showers.

WORDS OF WISDOM FROM
THE MOUTH OF GEORGE ANDERSON

- "I think firemen and what they do for a living, they're the real heroes in this world. We get paid outstanding money in baseball, and people ask for our autographs, but are you kidding me? We're not the heroes. When I go to a banquet and there are kids there, I stand up and tell them to get the autographs of the people who brought them to the banquet. Those people care far more about those kids than we do. We're there because we're paid. Those other people—fathers, mothers, uncles, and aunts—they brought those kids out, and they're the heroes."

- "The easiest thing in the world is to manage a team that's winning. They're all in a great frame of mind all the time. You can talk to them and tell them things you want them to know, and they will listen to you. You can get a lot of things done when you are winning. Losing, now that's different. That's the true test of you as an individual. When you are losing, you will find out which people you can depend on."

- "I figure God gave you class, and you have two choices of what to do with it. You can keep it, or you can give it away. When I see guys give it away with their behavior, they can never look anyone straight in the eye again. I wouldn't give it up if we finished in last place every year. I'll stand there and take my beatings. I can come back next year and try it

again because I didn't give up my class."

- "Baltimore is the class team in our division. That comes from tradition. Somewhere along the line, it gets down to where you have to beat Baltimore."

- "Whenever I eat right after a game, it's because I'm angry. I know that if I don't do something, I can say some nasty things—so I eat to keep my mouth full."

- "I make out my lineup the night before the game. I turn the TV on because I've gotta have sound in the room or I can't think. I gotta write the names down on a piece of paper because, if I don't see them, I can't start thinking about them."

- "If there is anything that bothers me about newspapers, it's the 'unnamed source.' When I read about an 'unnamed source,' I don't trust the writer. If you can't put a name to your comments, the comments aren't worth anything."

- "I never fear another manager. I never sit in my dugout and say, 'Oh, God, they have so-and-so over there.' All I care about is what players are over there and who's going to be playing tonight. They're the ones who can beat me."

- "The biggest mistake people make is when they bad-mouth people after they're fired. Once you bad-mouth people, you can't bring it back."

- "We live in a fake world. Baseball

isn't the real world, not like being a lawyer, a doctor, a plumber, an electrician, or a painter. It's a fairy-tale land and I can't believe it when some of our guys fall into the trap and believe our world is real."

- "I hear guys complaining about where they sit on the airplane. I don't get it. Will I get there any quicker if I sit in a different seat?"

- "My grandfather was a house painter. My daddy was a painter and my uncle was a painter—and, of course, that's what I should have done with my life. I like to paint. Nothing drastic can happen between you and the brush. When you paint, you can dream. And if you get into trouble, you can cover it up with the paint."

- "Players understand players better than anybody. If I want to get the right information on anyone, I go to the players. They know the ones with the courage, and they know the cowards."

- "I don't want my players to start blaming umpires for a loss. There might be an occasion now and then when the umpires might miss one. They also might give you one. I just think, if a player can learn that an umpire is not involved in the game, the player is a lot better off."

- "To me, there's nothing wrong with having a good debate with an umpire as long as you don't curse him. If you start cursing the man, you should be gone."

- "Umpires are so much more right than we are, it's unbelievable."

- "The only thing a manager can do

once the game starts is to make moves with his pitchers, and you're going to be good at that only if you have good pitchers."

- "Little things win in the long run. The big things take care of themselves. If the ball goes up in the stands, you can't do anything about it. They don't let you put fielders up there. But every time you have a runner on second base, he *has* to end up at least at third by the time you finish hitting."

- "I've made up my mind that it's wonderful to go to spring training and play golf. But if we have time to play golf, we're not getting our work done. If I hear about somebody playing golf, we'll just work a little longer, that's all."

- "I can understand people who boo us. You take a man who pays to go to the ballpark—that's no different from paying for a show. You expect to get entertainment, and he's upset if he doesn't get it. I don't blame him."

- "Some of the new ball parks are like plastic. They're beautiful, but you're not in contact with the fans. If I see a friend, I have to jump up to shake hands with him."

- "I like to see other managers happy when they win because I know what the feeling is."

- "I like wintertime. I can be with my kids. We make popcorn and watch college basketball. Those are great nights. Thank God, baseball is a million miles away on those nights."

- "I don't mind the fans yelling at us, as long as they don't shoot bullets. Bullets are serious."

- "The reason I keep my head down when I come back from the mound after changing pitchers? It's because the guy who is screaming at me might be my neighbor, and I don't want to know it."
- "The only time I get mad at the fans is when they use filthy language. You have to be a moron to use filthy language in the ballpark. There are a lot of morons around."
- "Some players think they are heroes because they put a uniform on. That doesn't make them heroes."
- "I can't believe they pay us for this—something we did for nothing as kids."

Sparky Anderson claims he is a very shy man—at home. It is another matter when he goes to work. He is not afraid to speak his mind when he thinks something goes wrong on the job. This sequence shows him giving a series of lectures to some of his favorite people.

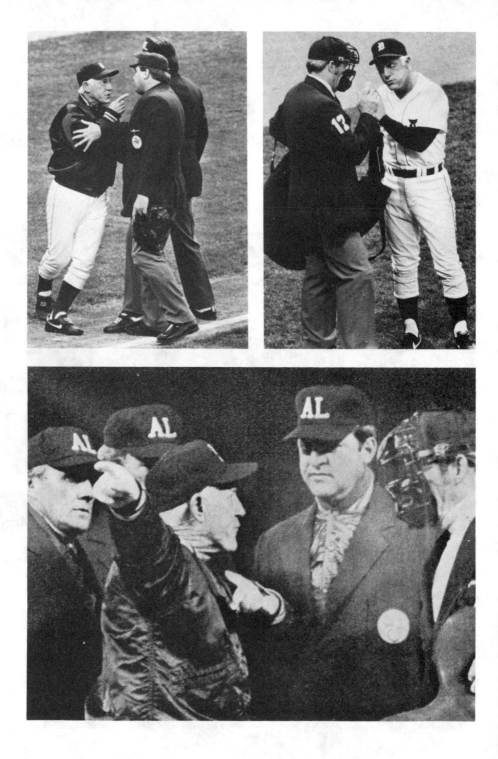

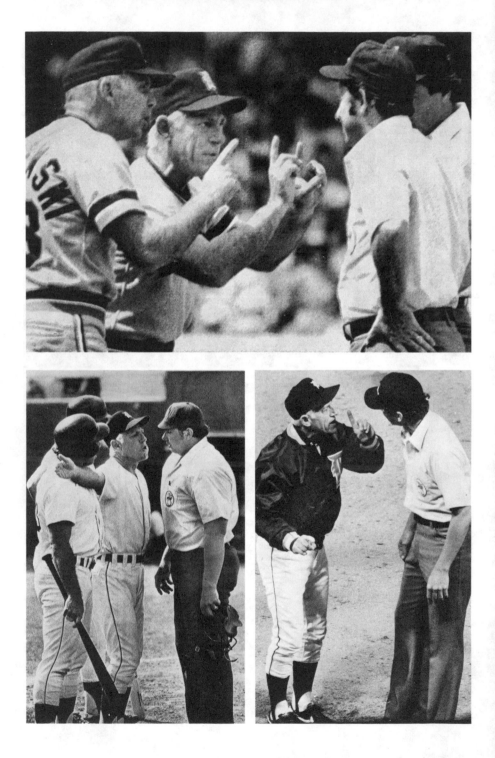

And another thing. . . .

JIM CAMPBELL REMEMBERS . . .

- His first night in baseball: The ballpark in Thomasville, Georgia, burned down. "I felt terrible about it—I just had the ladies' room fixed up with drapes, paint, and a new linoleum floor."

- When manager Charlie Dressen had his heart attack in spring training of 1965: "He didn't tell anybody about it. He got up early in the morning and had Stubby Overmire drive him to the airport in Tampa, and he flew clear across the country to see his doctor in Los Angeles. I remember he ate some chili the night before and complained of chest pains."

- The Detroit riot in 1967: "It started on a Sunday afternoon and I could see the guys in the press box going out on the roof to look at the smoke beyond the left-field stands. We didn't know what was going on. We went down to the waterfront and cooked some steaks and didn't learn about it until later in the night. The next day, only four of us showed up for work, and then the National Guard told us to go home."

- The death of Bob Swift in 1966: "He took over for Charlie Dressen and got cancer, and I remember sitting with him at the All-Star game in St. Louis. It was terribly hot there and the players were putting cool plates in their spikes to keep their feet from burning. We met Hoot Evers, and he took one look at Swiftie, an old friend, and said: 'What's wrong with him?' I told him, 'Nothing's wrong.' Hoot said, 'Bull—that man is sick.' I was with Bob almost every day and didn't see how he was failing."

- The 1972 player strike: "It happened on the last day of spring training, just as we were ready to come north. I went to the clubhouse and all the players were sitting around and I was really mad. I saw the truck outside, and it was filled with their bicycles and baby buggies. I stood in the middle of that room and let them have it. I looked at them and said, 'OK, you want this strike, you've got it. But Christmas is over. Santa Claus is dead. Go outside and get all those damned bikes and buggies off the truck.' Ever since then, every time I see Jim Northrup, he looks at me and grins, 'Aw, Santa Claus ain't dead.' "

- The Denny McLain trade in 1970: "Do you believe that 45 people were in on it—including a psychiatrist—and word never leaked out? We announced it at the World Series, with Bowie Kuhn presiding over the press conference. Some people accused us of upstaging the World Series. All I know is that a long, long ordeal was over, and when I went back to the hotel, I took a roll of Tums from my pocket and threw it in the street. I figured I didn't need them anymore."

- The sale of the Tigers to Tom Monaghan in 1983: "Another amazing story because 25 people

Puzzle Picture: Who is this handsome devil with all that hair? (It's none other than Jim Campbell in his college days.)

knew it—all kinds of lawyers, bankers, and their secretaries—and again nothing leaked out."

- The day California knocked the Tigers out of the pennant in the final game of the 1967 season: "I can't ever remember a worse day in the ballpark. We lost and the fans started tearing up the stadium. I called Bill Rigney in the California clubhouse and said:

'Rig, if you proved nothing today, you proved how honest this game is. Your guys didn't have a thing at stake, but they fought us all the way. I thank you.'"

- The night they burned the police car after the 1984 World Series: "I've always said, and still do, if they hadn't burned that police car, it wouldn't have been called a riot. I remember standing in my office when somebody threw a Coca-Cola bottle through the window. It almost hit John Fetzer. Can you imagine how embarrassing that was? We were there with Millie Schembechler, the governor's wife, Peter Ueberroth and his wife, and here comes a bottle smashing through the window? But I'll tell you something, the fans downstairs caught the guy who threw it and held him for the police. A lot of bad things were happening out there and a few good things."

- The night the ballpark burned in 1974, destroying the press box: "I'm at home watching the national news from New York and here comes a bulletin—the guy says Tiger Stadium is on fire. I open the drapes of my high-rise and I can see the glow in the skies."

- Trades: "Do you believe that I once tried to trade Mickey Lolich for Dick Howser? That's when Mickey Lolich was coming up through the farm system. That's how smart I was."

- His association with John Fetzer: "Not once in all the years I worked for this man did he ever second-guess me. The toughest he ever got was, 'Maybe next time, you ought to consider this.' Wait, I take it back. He was always after me about my weight."

Opening Day . . . and the man who runs the Tigers is there with the man who runs the city.

INSIDE DARRELL EVANS

Favorite food: Anything Mexican, especially tacos. Absolutely won't eat Brussels sprouts or cauliflower.

Descent: Welsh-German-Mexican-Indian.

Family: His mother Eleanor was one of the finest softball players in Pasadena in the 1940s and 1950s.

The first thing he and his wife did when they got to Detroit: Go to a Red Wings hockey game.

Most bizarre experience: In July 1982 he sighted a UFO outside his home in Livermore, California. "It was triangle-shaped with a

Darrell Evans and Chad Richard (August 16, 1985).

wing span of about 30 feet, with a line of red and green lights and a bank of white lights in the back." He went into the house to get a camera, but when he returned, "the thing took off like it was going a million miles an hour." Yes, he would have liked to have gone with it. "I am a very optimistic person, so I believe we will discover that somebody else is out there before this generation ends."

Favorite movie: Close Encounters of the Third Kind.

Hobbies: Fishing and tennis.

Favorite TV shows: "Miami Vice," "Hill Street Blues," and "Cheers."

Darrell Evans also loves a parade, but whatever became of Barbero Garbey?

Timely hit: When Darrell Evans smacked his 300th major-league homer, he did it at 3:00 P.M. on a 3-and-0 pitch.

Former job: Worked as mail carrier (used to save stamps).

Player he admires most: Hank Aaron.

Biggest thrill in baseball: Being on base when Aaron hit his 715th home run.

Little-known fact: He wears contact lenses.

Childhood: A big Dodger fan when he was a kid. He lived 15 minutes from the ballpark and would go to 40 games a year. Yes, he hated the San Francisco Giants, a team he later played for.

Nickname: He was known as "Doody," for Howdy Doody, when he played for the Giants, but nobody uses it in Detroit.

Home: A seven-bedroom house in Grosse Pointe.

BEST SHOPPING CITY

Dick Tracewski's favorite shopping city on afternoons of night games:

- *New York*—"I love it along Delancey Street in lower Manhattan. You can buy anything there, from grapefruits to sneakers. It's a great feeling to eat grapefruits in your sneakers."

WORST JOBS

- *Tom Brookens:* "The worst job I ever had was looking for a job. I couldn't find one. I was terrible at it."
- *Darrell Evans:* "Pulling 150 acres worth of weeds."
- *Lance Parrish:* "Tarring roofs."
- *Dave Bergman:* "Packing fish on Cape Cod. I stank all summer."
- *Milt Wilcox:* "The midnight shift in an oil field."
- *Dan Petry:* "My mom's paper route. She had 300 customers."

Kirk Gibson does sign autographs. Sometimes.

INSIDE DAN PETRY

Favorite drink: Root beer float.

Nickname: "Peaches." "When they call you 'Peaches,' " he says, "you'd better have a sense of humor."

Milestone: He made history on December 5, 1983, when he became the highest-paid player in Tiger history, up to that time, when he agreed to a four-year contract worth more than $3.5 million.

Clothing: With all his money, he wears Levis. "I'm not one for designer jeans."

Favorite colors: Blue and green. "I like the outdoors, and those are outdoor colors."

The person he'd most like to meet: Jack Nicklaus.

Favorite city: San Francisco. "I like to walk around Fisherman's Wharf, with all the shops."

Least favorite city: Montgomery, Alabama. "It's the pits, a boring and dead town."

Similarity to Jack Morris: They both throw right-handed, they both have mustaches, and they both have the same agent, Dick Moss.

Dan Petry masters the snowball.

How he learned to relax on the pitcher's mound: By going to a specialist who taught him "creative relaxation."

Boyhood idols: Nolan Ryan and James Dean.

Favorite number: Four.

Political affiliations: None.

Class act: When the Kansas City Royals charged him with deliberately hitting Willie Wilson in the face with a pitch, Petry sent Wilson a telegram apologizing. The telegram said: "Willie: I

Dan Petry: pitcher at work.

am sorry. It was truly unintentional. My sincere apologies. Dan Petry."

Hobby: The study of astronomy.

How he describes himself: "Nobody's interested in me. I'm boring. Coach Dick Tracewski voted me the most boring guy on the club."

Biggest turn-on: The feeling of winning a major-league game.

Biggest turnoff: Selfish people.

Favorite school subjects: Math and science.

Favorite book: Catcher in the Rye.

Ambition: He wanted to be an outfielder.

How his career started: 0-5 at Lakeland.

How he was born: Very carefully. His mother had had three miscarriages and nearly miscarried him. As a baby, he suffered from severe bronchitis and a heart murmur.

Most memorable moment: Winning the baseball championship in high school.

BEST AND WORST ELEVATORS

Alex Grammas's favorite and least favorite elevators:

WORST

1. *San Diego*—"First of all, I hate elevators, but I hate the elevators in San Diego most of all. They never show up. And when they do, they either don't move or they move so slowly you can feel your armpits getting wet."

2. *New York*—"Absolutely the worst elevators in the world. I'll never get on them alone. Even when I'm alone, I'll walk down the corridors backward to make sure nobody is following me."

BEST

1. *Kansas City*—"I like the windows in the elevators. You can look out and see the stockyards, but you can't smell them."

2. *Toronto*—"For international elevators, they're not bad. But give me a good escalator anytime.

Comment: "I have claustrophobia. I wonder if Alfred Hitchcock would like to make a movie about me?"

IF IACOCCA OWNED THE TIGERS

Some people say Lee Iacocca, boss of the Chrysler Corporation, would make a good president of the United States.

Heck, he would make a good sportswriter.

Here are some excerpts from his book, *Iacocca: An Autobiography* (Bantam, 1985), that could be applied to certain Tigers:

- *To Kirk Gibson*—"I think all the talent in the world doesn't excuse rudeness."
- *To Gates Brown*—"Mistakes are a part of life; you can't avoid them. All you can hope is that they won't be too expensive and that you don't make the same mistake twice."
- *To Jim Campbell*—"I'm constantly amazed by the number of people who can't control their own schedules. Over the years, I've had many executives come to me and say with pride, 'Boy, last year I worked so hard that I didn't take any vacation.' It's actually nothing to be proud of. I always feel like responding: 'You dummy. You mean to tell me you can take the responsibility for an $80 million project and you can't plan to take two weeks out of the year and go off and have some fun?' "
- *To Dan Petry*—"Setbacks are a natural part of life, and you've got to be careful how you respond to them. You can't sulk too long."
- *To Sparky Anderson*—"If I had to sum up in one word the qualities that make a good manager, I'd say that it all comes down to decisiveness. And I don't mean to act rashly."
- *To Billy Muffett*—"The only way you can motivate people is to communicate with them."
- *To Bill Lajoie*—"When you give a guy a raise, that's the time to increase his responsibilities. While he's in a good frame of mind, you reward him for what he's done and, at the same time, you motivate him to do even more. Always hit him while he's up, and never be too tough on him when he's down."
- *To Lance Parrish*—"Leadership means setting an example. When you find yourself in a position of leadership, people follow your every move. So you have to be careful about everything you say and everything you do."
- *To Jack Morris's agent*—"I want labor to understand the inner workings of management. The economic future depends on increased cooperation between union and management. Only by working together can we take on the world."
- *To Tom Monaghan*—"I'm a strong believer in the dignity of labor. As far as I'm concerned, working people should be well paid for their time and effort. I'm certainly not a socialist, but I am in favor of sharing the wealth—so long as the company is making money."

INSIDE LARRY HERNDON

Larry Herndon is uncomfortable talking in public, especially about himself. We respect that.

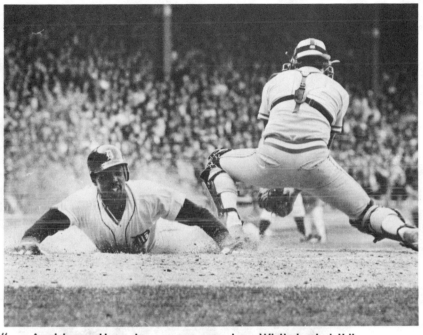

". . . And Larry Herndon scores on Lou Whitaker's hit."

BEST MANAGERS

Sparky Anderson's three favorite managers:

1. *Casey Stengel*—"He was the greatest publicity man baseball has ever known. He *was* baseball."
2. *Charlie Dressen*—"A brilliant mind. They also tell me he could make a good bowl of chili."
3. *Walter Alston*—"He never changed. He knew how to run a ball club."

INSIDE WALT TERRELL

Childhood home: A three-room house ("not a three-bedroom house, a three-room house") in Jeffersonville, Indiana.

Favorite food: Anything his mom cooks because he knows what he is getting. "When you eat out, they turn the lights out and you never know what they're bringing you." Exception: A double Wendy's with everything.

Married: Karen Forge, an expert volleyball player.

Special treat: Popsicles.

Least favorite city: Any big·city. "I just don't like being in a hurry."

Hobbies: Fishing, golfing, racquetball, and shooting pool. "I'm not a pool shark, but I could beat Bill Scherer."

Milestone: He once hit two home runs in a game, connecting off Ferguson Jenkins in Wrigley Field.

Pet peeves: U.S. giving away money to other countries "when we've got needy people in our country." Also, people who flaunt money. "I see some guys with so much gold around their neck,

Walt Terrell and the gang at home in Ft. Thomas, Kentucky. That's Mike on his lap, Erin sitting with mom, Karen, and Ryan on the right.

they can't stand up straight." Finally, batters who keep stepping out of the batter's box.

Ambition: To own his own bowling machine—the kind they have in bars.

Favorite movie: None. Doesn't like movies. His wife falls asleep at them and he hates to pay $5 to watch her sleep. "She can do that at home for nothing."

Favorite books: Dr. Seuss books. He has read them 10,000 times, at a conservative estimate, to his three small children.

Tiger Stadium Bleacher Bums.

THE OWNER SPEAKS

Tom Monaghan bought the Tigers in the autumn of 1983. He did it because he has always loved the Tigers and because he could afford it. The purchase price was $53 million.

Monaghan, 48, is a self-made man who took a single pizza store in Ypsilanti, Michigan, and turned it into the world's largest pizza delivery chain—Domino's.

You heard it here first:

All mine. . . .

- "I'm thinking about putting the green seats back in Tiger Stadium. I don't know why they took them out of there in the first place."
- "As long as I own this team, we will not build a new stadium. I like the old stadium, and we'll do all we can to keep it. We'll keep fixing it up and making it look as good as possible. I even like the way the posts look. It gives a good feeling to the ballpark. It reminds me of the stadium at Cooperstown. I'll probably take the posts out one day, but I don't want to."
- "I still can't believe John Fetzer sold the team to me."
- "People tell me the outside of our stadium looks good. It's a joke. All they've done is cover it up with a lot of tin. I'd like to strip it right down to its natural concrete base and grow ivy on the walls. That would look beautiful."
- "I don't understand why players can't bunt the ball. All you have to do is move your arms around a little and put the bat on the ball. That doesn't seem so difficult to me."
- "When I grew up in an orphanage, the only fun we had was listening to the Tigers on the radio. That's why I can't believe I own the team."
- "It really is easy dropping down a bunt."

Monaghan's pizza-copter.

In honor of Sparky Anderson, the Dave Bergman family has a guinea pig named Sparky.

WHERE'S HOME PLATE?

Ernie Harwell's favorite restaurants in American League cities:

1. *Milwaukee:* English Room of Pfister Hotel, for veal piccata.
2. *Baltimore:* Hausner's, for crab flakes au gratin.
3. *New York:* D'Angelo's, for clams casino and fettuccine Alfredo.
4. *Toronto:* Barberians, for filet mignon.
5. *San Francisco–Oakland:* Washington Square Bar & Grille, for trout Prestalli.
6. *Cleveland:* Swingo's, for steak au poivre.
7. *Anaheim:* Acapulco, for gazpacho and nachos—the hotter, the better.
8. *Kansas City:* Stephenson's Apple Farm, for brisket of beef and apple fritters.
9. *Detroit:* Pontchartrain Wine Cellars, for perch.
10. *Boston:* Half Shell, for scrod.

INSIDE TOM BROOKENS

Family: He was a twin, born three minutes apart from his brother Tim. Tim tried to make it with the Texas Rangers' club but is back in Fayetteville, teaching school.

Married: Christa Schoenfelt, New Year's Eve.

Hobbies: Hunting, fishing, darts, and chopping wood. "Don't laugh at chopping wood—I love it. I'll cut up to 25 cords each winter."

Favorite food: Homemade pot pies—ham, chicken, or beef. Won't eat sauerkraut.

Wyatt Earp, who looks an awful lot like Tom Brookens.

Favorite color: Blue (as in blue jeans).

Favorite city: Denver. "I like the mountains."

Home: A farmhouse built in 1888 in Fayetteville, Pennsylvania, not far from Gettysburg.

Biggest turn-on: "Spending time with my wife."

Biggest turnoff: Pushy people.

Favorite TV show: "Saturday Night Live."

Pet peeve: "People who don't use turn signals."

Toughest pitcher: Danny Darwin.

Favorite book: None. "I don't read too many books."

People he most admires: Mother and father.

Athletic background: Never made high school football or basketball team.

"I know your bat is sick but I don't think they'll let you put these bandages on it."

Rick Ferrell, the longtime scout, is the checkers champion of the Tigers. But he'll give you a chance to beat him. "I'll play you left-handed," says Ferrell.

INSIDE ALAN TRAMMELL

Favorite color: Green. It reminds him of money and grass, and he likes both of them.

Major-league initiation: He played his first game in the major leagues when he was only 20 years old, before he could vote. That made him the youngest player in the major leagues.

First hit: It came off Reggie Cleveland in Boston. It was a single up the middle. They stopped the game and gave him the ball.

Favorite singer/rock group: Led Zeppelin. "But," he says, "that's when I was young."

Boyhood idol: Willie Mays.

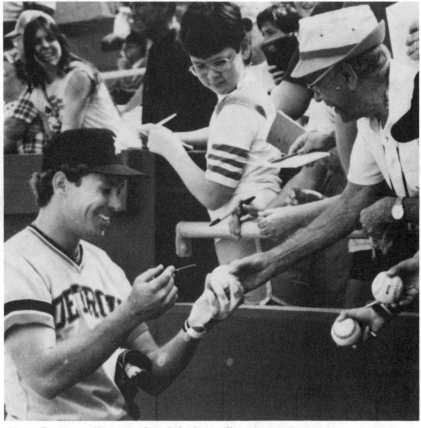

Alan Trammell: everybody's favorite.

Lucky number: Three.

Memory of the minor leagues: "They had no grounds crew at Columbus, Georgia, and we had to go out and rake and water the field before the games. They had boulder-sized rocks out there and you didn't dare slide or you'd get killed."

Biggest turnoff: Nosy people.

Childhood: He drew strike zones on the garage door and on a chimney on the back of house, pretended he was a pitcher, and threw a tennis ball at them. Two days after graduating from high school, "I was playing in the minor leagues. Baseball was all I ever wanted to do with my life."

Favorite TV show: "M*A*S*H"

Favorite book: *The Jackie Robinson Story.*

Person he admires most: Al Kaline.

Craziest injury: When he got dressed as Frankenstein on Halloween and fell down the stairs, injuring his knee.

Why he didn't tip his hat on his two World Series homers in 1984: "I don't like to show anyone up—that's not my style."

On beating San Diego in the World Series: "It felt strange because I used to sneak under the fence when I was a kid to watch them play."

On Lou Whitaker: "A natural. Frank White is the smartest player in our league and Lou is going to take his place."

On the blue seats in Tiger Stadium: "I liked the green ones better."

On snow: "Terrible. It looks pretty through the window, but pretty terrible through your car window."

On curve balls: "You gotta hang in there."

On marriage: "You gotta hang in there."

Wife Barbara says: "Alan is good around the house. We almost never talk baseball. I don't know whether he wins or loses. We just don't talk about it."

Trainer Jack Homel: "How do you get a dub-dub in shape?"
Reporter: "I give up."
Homel: "You rub a dub-dub."

INSIDE LOU WHITAKER

Favorite color: Green. "It's the color of money."

Lou and Asia.

Childhood home: Born in Brooklyn, but grew up in Martinsville, Virginia, with 20 people in his home. He had a bedroom in the basement with his brother. His mom worked nights at a drive-in restaurant (5:00 P.M. until midnight), and he would wait up for her because "she always had goodies for us."

Favorite city: Baltimore. "It's close to my home."

Least favorite city: "The entire West Coast."

Childhood affliction: His legs grew outward to make him bowlegged. His family couldn't afford braces or crutches, so his uncle would turn his legs in every night and hope they would grow straight. They did. In school, he wore weights on his legs to strengthen them.

Nickname: "Sweet Lou," but when he was a kid, they called him "Tippy Toes" because of his bowlegs. He hated the name.

Religion: Jehovah's Witness. It is very important to him, and he and teammate Chet Lemon will not remain on the field during the playing of the National Anthem because they cannot answer to any being except their own God.

Favorite school subject: Math.

Best time: Playing in the park with his family.

Before becoming a ball player: He never saw a professional game.

Learned the game: By playing with a rubber ball and a stick.

Alternate career: If he wasn't a player, he'd be a singer. "I used to sing in the choir when I was growing up, and I used to sing good."

High fives for Lou Whitaker after a three-run homer.

Nothing was tough about growing up. I was mature at the age of 12. My grandmother taught me to be quiet and just listen. She said you never learned anything talking.

> —Lou Whitaker, on the toughest part of growing up

Marty Castillo on the most scared he has ever been in his life: "It was in Kansas City. The players started throwing grasshoppers on me. I can't stand grasshoppers. They were in my clothes and in my shoes. I was terrified."

Bill Scherrer on why he never had a pet rock: "They have to die someday, and I don't like to see anything die."

This is the world's greatest ballpark and it is situated near the heart of the world's greatest city. Who's prejudiced?